STANDARDS FOR ADULT LOCAL DETENTION FACILITIES
Third Edition

American Correctional Association
In cooperation with the
Commission on Accreditation for Corrections

March 1991

Standards Manuals Published by the American Correctional Association

Standards for the Administration of Correctional Agencies
Standards for Adult Community Residential Services
Standards for Adult Correctional Boot Camp Programs
Standards for Adult Correctional Institutions
Standards for Adult Local Detention Facilities
Standards for Adult Parole Authorities
Standards for Adult Probation and Parole Field Services
Standards for Correctional Industries
Standards for Correctional Training Academies
Standards for Electronic Monitoring Programs
Standards for Juvenile Community Residential Facilities
Standards for Juvenile Correctional Boot Camp Programs
Standards for Juvenile Day Treatment Programs
Standards for Juvenile Detention Facilities
Standards for Juvenile Probation and Aftercare Services
Standards for Juvenile Training Schools
Standards for Small Juvenile Detention Facilities
Standards for Small Jail Facilities
Certification Standards for Food Service Programs
Certification Standards for Health Care Programs
Foundation/Core Standards for Adult Community Residential Services
Foundation/Core Standards for Adult Correctional Institutions
Foundation/Core Standards for Adult Local Detention Facilities

Accredited facilities on the cover:

Top left, Hunterdon County Jail, Flemington, NJ
Top right, Hennepin County Adult Corrections Facility, Plymouth, MN
Bottom left, Fairfax County Adult Detention Center, Fairfax, VA
Bottom right, Hillsborough County Jail-Central, Tampa, FL
Center, Hillsborough County Jail-West, Tampa, FL

Information on accreditation may be obtained from:

American Correctional Association
Department of Standards and Accreditation
4380 Forbes Blvd.
Lanham, MD 20706-4322
(301) 918-1835

American Correctional Association:

James A. Gondles, Jr., Executive Director
Robert Verdeyen, Director, Standards and Accreditation
Gabriella Daley, Director, Communications and Publications
Leslie A. Maxam, Assistant Director, Communications and Publications
Alice Fins, Publications Managing Editor
Michael Kelly, Associate Editor
Mike Selby, Production Editor

Copyright 1991 by the American Correctional Association. Reprinted 1998 by TechniGraphix, Reston, Va. All rights reserved. The reproduction, distribution, or inclusion in other publications of materials in this book is prohibited without prior written permission from the American Correctional Association. No part of this book may be reproduced by any electronic means, including information storage and retrieval systems, without permission in writing from the publisher.

ISBN 0-929310-47-0

COMMISSION ON ACCREDITATION FOR CORRECTIONS

Board of Commissioners

M. Wayne Huggins, Virginia, Chair
Perry M. Johnson, Michigan, Vice Chair
Norman E. Wirkler, Colorado, Member-at-Large
Marjorie H. Young, Georgia, Member-at-Large
Victoria C. Myers, Missouri, Member-at-Large

James W. Black, Colorado
Robert L. Brutsche, Virginia
Penelope D. Clute, New York
Raymond J. Coleman, Washington
John A. Corcoros, Texas
Jacqueline Crawford, Arizona
David C. Evans, Georgia
Bonnie L. Hays, Oregon
James M. Jordan, Illinois
Orlando L. Martinez, Colorado
John Minor, Michigan
Jay M. Newberger, South Dakota
Frank A. Orlando, Florida
George M. Phyfer, Alabama
Luke Quinn, Michigan
Virginia Swanson, Washington

AMERICAN CORRECTIONAL ASSOCIATION

Samuel Sublett, Jr., Illinois, President
Helen G. Corrothers, District of Columbia, President-Elect
Su Cunningham, Texas, Past President
J. Bryan Riley, Massachusetts, Vice President
Bobbie L. Huskey, Illinois, Treasurer
Anthony P. Travisono, Executive Director

Board of Governors

Dennis S. Avery, Minnesota
Judy Culpepper Briscoe, Texas
Robert Brown, Jr., Michigan
Fred L. Crawford, Florida
Pamela Jo Davis, Florida
Larry L. Dye, New York
Ana I. Gispert, Florida
James A. Gondles, Jr., Virginia
Michael J. Mahoney, Illinois
William V. Milliken, Florida

JoAnn Longo Nelson, Washington
Donald M. Page, Canada
J. Michael Quinlan, District of Columbia
Linda D'Amario Rossi, Maryland
David W. Roush, Michigan
Chiquita A. Sipos, California
Ronald L. Stepanik, Florida
Robert J. Watson, Delaware
Bruce I. Wolford, Kentucky

Committee on Standards

James R. Irving, Illinois, *Chair*

Thomas Albrecht, District of Columbia
Fred Allen, New York
James W. Black, Colorado
Robert Brown, Jr., Michigan
Robert L. Brutsche, Virginia
Penelope D. Clute, New York
Thomas A. Coughlin III, New York
Jacqueline Crawford, Arizona
Pamela Jo Davis, Florida
David C. Evans, Georgia

Harold A. Farrier, Iowa
Susan Humphrey-Barnett, Alaska
Perry M. Johnson, Michigan
Gary D. Maynard, Oklahoma
J. Michael Quinlan, District of Columbia
John D. Rees, New Mexico
Virginia Swanson, Washington
George W. Wilson, Ohio
Norman E. Wirkler, Colorado

Standards and Accreditation Staff

W. Hardy Rauch, *Director*
Jeffrey Washington, *Administrator*
Karen Kushner, *Regional Administrator*
Kevin Ashburn, *Regional Administrator*
Robert Verdeyen, *Regional Administrator*
Ken Neagle, *Regional Administrator*
Christine Pacanowski, *PIE Associate Project Coordinator*
Sue Tuller, *Assistant Regional Administrator*
Carol Swahl, *Office Manager*
Karen Smalley, *Accounting Officer*
Joy Callies, *Executive Assistant*
Grace Medley, *Staff Assistant*
Deborah Butler, *Staff Assistant*
Debbie Shaw, *Staff Assistant*

STANDARDS FOR ADULT LOCAL DETENTION FACILITIES

Totals of Weights

Category   *Number*

Mandatory Standards   35
Nonmandatory Standards   386

Summary of Mandatory Standards

3-ALDF-1D-18	Training and Staff Development
3-ALDF-1D-19	Training and Staff Development
3-ALDF-2A-02	Building and Safety Codes
3-ALDF-2G-05	Security
3-ALDF-3A-29	Security and Control
3-ALDF-3A-31	Security and Control
3-ALDF-3A-32	Security and Control
3-ALDF-3B-01	Safety and Emergency Procedures
3-ALDF-3B-02	Safety and Emergency Procedures
3-ALDF-3B-03	Safety and Emergency Procedures
3-ALDF-3B-04	Safety and Emergency Procedures
3-ALDF-3B-05	Safety and Emergency Procedures
3-ALDF-3B-10	Safety and Emergency Procedures
3-ALDF-3B-11	Safety and Emergency Procedures
3-ALDF-3B-12	Safety and Emergency Procedures
3-ALDF-3B-14	Safety and Emergency Procedures
3-ALDF-3E-08	Inmate Rights
3-ALDF-4C-04	Food Service
3-ALDF-4C-06	Food Service
3-ALDF-4C-09	Food Service
3-ALDF-4C-11	Food Service
3-ALDF-4C-13	Food Service
3-ALDF-4D-01	Sanitation and Hygiene
3-ALDF-4D-02	Sanitation and Hygiene
3-ALDF-4D-03	Sanitation and Hygiene
3-ALDF-4D-04	Sanitation and Hygiene
3-ALDF-4E-02	Health Care
3-ALDF-4E-09	Health Care
3-ALDF-4E-10	Health Care
3-ALDF-4E-17	Health Care
3-ALDF-4E-19	Health Care
3-ALDF-4E-20	Health Care
3-ALDF-4E-21	Health Care
3-ALDF-4E-43	Health Care
3-ALDF-5A-13	Work and Correctional Industries

Foreword

This publication is the third edition manual of standards produced by the American Correctional Association for adult local detention facilities. The first Manual of Standards for Adult Detention Facilities, published in December 1977, has served as the foundation for accreditation activities involving a number of detention facilities throughout the nation.

That edition was followed by a second edition in 1981. This third manual reflects the Association's commitment to continually review and update standards to ensure that they reflect the current professional requirements in the field of corrections. Over 300 national and international leaders representing all facets of the correctional scene have contributed to and participated in the development and revision of these standards. These standards are frequently referred to by the executive, legislative, and judicial branches of local, state, and federal jurisdictions as the professional benchmark for judging the quality of a detention operation. The revision process is a function of the ACA Committee on Standards, conducted in cooperation with the Commission on Accreditation for Corrections, ACA affiliates, and law enforcement agencies.

Special Needs of Local Detention Facilities

The need for a set of national standards detailing minimum operational practice has long been recognized by public officials responsible for the administration of local detention facilities. The detention function includes the custody and care of those persons accused but not convicted of a crime and of those sentenced as a disposition following conviction of criminal acts.

Local detention facilities are unique to corrections for a variety of reasons: (1) they are operated most often by local jurisdictions, not statewide agencies; (2) they are often operated by a law enforcement official, i.e., police chief or sheriff, rather than a correctional administrator; (3) their role as a secure facility for pretrial detainees is different from that of a long-term institution (intake and classification procedures require greater focus on security and the separation of various types of offenders); and (4) the programs and services of the local detention facility place greater emphasis on short-term detention and offender involvement with the community.

Detention facility programs must also respond to a variety of special needs of detainees and inmates. Local detention facilities house pretrial detainees, thereby holding individuals who are presumed innocent yet require maximum security prior to trial; witnesses; civil prisoners; and other types of detainees. This creates unique problems for detention facility personnel. For instance, detention facility operation requires the separate management of pretrial and unsentenced persons, work releasees, weekenders, trustees, and inmates with special problems (alcohol and drug abusers, the mentally disturbed, the physically handicapped), as well as women and juveniles if they are held in the same facility. Programs of pretrial diversion frequently offered in detention facilities also require special procedures and resources. Admission procedures in detention facilities must provide for greater contact with family, legal counsel, bonding persons, and others in the community.

In developing standards for detention facilities, the varied and complex roles of the facility and its staff had to be evaluated. It was also necessary to consider that detention facility populations are controlled more by statute and court practices than by the size of the jurisdiction that maintains the facility. Variations in law enforcement practices, availability of alternatives such as detoxification centers, release on recognizance programs, misdemeanant diversion and similar programs, and attitudes of the local citizens also affect jail admissions and the programs available in the community. With these concerns in mind, the standards have been developed and subsequently revised in this third edition.

The contents of this manual then, like those of its predecessors, emerge from a thoughtful process of debate and deliberation. The decisions reached continue to represent the best consensus of professionals in the field. Members of the Committee on Standards have made every effort to found their work on relevant court decisions and good correctional practice. It is hoped this effort will assist in informing the courts, as well as legislators and governors, of the needs of corrections professionals who direct the increasingly complex administration of safe and humane institutions while also trying to provide meaningful services and programs for offenders.

Categories

The wide variance of size and function of local detention facilities does require clarification for standards application.

Generally speaking, there are three major categories of jails. The first is the general purpose detention facility or jail. Usually a city or county facility that detains persons for more than 48 hours, it is used both as a detention center for persons facing criminal charges and as a correctional facility for persons convicted of misdemeanor and felony crimes. Although this varies by jurisdiction, such a facility may retain a convicted offender for up to one year, while providing comprehensive care and services for the entire inmate population. In some jurisdictions there are local branch facilities for offenders with long-term sentences and honor camps or farms for minimum security inmates. For purposes of standards and accreditation, these facilities are grouped into the category "Detention."

The second category is the holding or lockup facility where arrestees are usually detained up to 48 hours, excluding holidays and weekends. These temporary holding facilities frequently are located in city police stations and county sheriffs' departments. Concerned primarily with the reception and temporary detention of persons awaiting arraignment and disposition or transfer to other authorities, lockups and holding facilities are not expected to provide the range of services found in the general purpose jail. For purposes of standards and accreditation, these facilities are grouped in the category "Holding."

The third category of local detention facilities is one that contains a mixture of long-term, short-term, and holding units. This condition often exists because of state legislation that enables, or requires, local facilities to house inmates for up to six years. In these facilities, it is necessary to combine standards designed for long-term facilities (Adult Correctional Institutions) with the standards intended for local detention facilities. These "hybrid" standards are developed by the ACA staff in close coordination with the facility to be accredited.

Acknowledgements

Special appreciation is extended to all of the members of the ACA Standards Committee and to other professional associations, including the National Sheriffs Association, American Jail Association, American Bar Association, American Medical Association, American Institute of Architects, and the National Association of Counties.

The ACA Standards and Accreditation staff were responsible for drafting, editing, and reviewing this edition to ensure that the manual is representative of the seven-year revision process.

Task Force Participants and Reviewers:

Larry R. Ard	Norma Lammers
James Black	Calvin Lightfoot
David Bogard	Charles B. Meeks
Robert L. Brutsche, M.D.	Dean N. Moser, Jr.
James H. Dunning	Carl R. Peed
Francis R. Ford	J. Michael Quinlan
James A. Gondles, Jr.	Walter Ridley
Frank A. Hall	L. John Simonet
Sara Heatherly	Ed Tripp
Frank W. Henn	Robert Viterna
M. Wayne Huggins	Norman E. Wirkler
Susan Humphrey-Barnett	

Foreword

The Commission on Accreditation for Corrections staff, under the direction of Hardy Rauch, have contributed significantly to the revision process and the publication of these standards. Jeffrey Washington and Kevin Ashburn served as the Commission's principal staff members in the revision effort, providing the coordination vital to the approval process.

Resource Agencies

National Institute of Corrections, *M. Wayne Huggins, Director*

Bureau of Justice Assistance, *William F. Powers, Director*

National Institute of Justice, *Charles DeWitt, Director*

Jail Center, *Michael O'Toole, Director*

The Detention Reporter, *Rod Miller, Editor*

American Jail Association, *Hagerstown, Maryland*

National Sheriffs Association, *Alexandria, Virginia*

ACA Adult Local Detention Committee

Department of Justice, Federal Bureau of Prisons

Georgia Department of Corrections

Lucas County Correction Center, *Toledo, Ohio*

Lafayette Parish Correctional Center, *Lafayette, Louisiana*

Hillsborough County Sheriff's Office, *Tampa, Florida*

Douglas County Jail, *Douglasville, Georgia*

Corrections Corporation of American, *Nashville, Tennessee*

Wackenhut Corrections Corporation, *Coral Gables, Florida*

Arlington County Detention Center, *Arlington, Virginia*

Alexandria Detention Center, *Alexandria, Virginia*

Fairfax County Adult Detention Center, *Fairfax, Virginia*

Contra Costa County Detention Center, *Martinez, California*

Denver County Jail and Pre-Arraignment Facility, *Denver, Colorado*

Multnomah County Detention Center, *Portland, Oregon*

Palm Beach County Detention Center, *West Palm Beach, Florida*

Montgomery County Detention Center, *Rockville, Maryland*

Contents

Foreword vi
Introduction to Accreditation xvi

Part I
Administration and Management 3-ALDF-1A-01—1G-09

Section A
General Administration
    Purpose and Mission 1
    Policy and Goal Formulation 1
    Appointed Personnel 2
    Qualifications 2
    Term of Office 3
    Table of Organization 3
    Policy and Procedure Manuals 3
    Channels of Communication 4
    Monitoring and Assessment 4
    Media Access 5
    Legal Counsel 5
    Political Practices 5

Section B
Fiscal Management
    Fiscal Control 7
    Accounting Procedures 7
    Cash Management 8
    Internal Monitoring 8
    Independent Audit 8
    Inventory 8
    Purchasing 9
    Community Services 9
    Position Control 9
    Institutional Insurance 9
    Commissary/Canteen 10
    Inmate Funds 10

Section C
Personnel
    Personnel Policy Manual 11
    Staffing Requirements 12
    Equal Employment Opportunity 13
    Selection and Promotion 13
    Probationary Term 13
    Provisional Appointments 13
    Criminal Record Check 14
    Physical Examination 14
    Drug-free Workplace 14
    Performance Reviews 15
    Compensation and Benefits 15
    Personnel Files 16
    Code of Ethics 16

Contents

    Confidentiality of Information 16
    Employee Assistance Program 16

Section D
Training and Staff Development

    Training 17
    Training Resources 17
    Outside Resources 17
    Training Plan 18
    Space and Equipment 18
    Reimbursement 18
    Training Requirements 19
    Administrative Staff 20
    Support Staff 20
    Part-time Staff 20
    Specialized Training 20
    Use of Force 21
    Use of Firearms 21
    Use of Chemical Agents 21
    Continuing Education 21

Section E
Case Records

    Case Record Management 23
    Transfer of Records 23
    Computation of Time Served 23
    Inmate Access to Records 23
    Release of Information 24

Section F
Information System and Research

    Information System 25
    Sharing of Information 25
    Master Index and Daily Reports 25
    Conduct of Research 27
    Inmate Participation 27

Section G
Citizen Involvement and Volunteers

    Program Coordination 28
    Screening and Selection 28
    Registration 28
    Offer of Professional Services 29
    Orientation and Training 29
    Schedule of Services 29
    Participation in Policy Making 29

Part Two
Physical Plant 3-ALDF-2A-01—2G-05

Section A
Building and Safety Codes
    Building Codes 31
    Fire Codes 31

Section B
Size, Organization, and Location
    Staff/Inmate Interaction 32
    Unit Size 32
    Rated Capacity 32
    Location 33

Section C
Inmate Housing
    Inmate Sleeping Areas 34
    Furnishings 34
    Existing Renovation, Addition, New Plant 34
    Space Requirements 35
    Toilets 36
    Wash Basins 36
    Showers 36
    Special Management Housing 37
    Housing for the Handicapped 37

Section D
Environmental Conditions
    Light Levels 38
    Inmate Rooms/Cells 38
    Natural Light 38
    Day Rooms 39
    Indoor Air Quality 39
    Heating and Cooling 39

Section E
Program and Service Areas
    Exercise and Recreation 40
    Visiting 41
    Classrooms 41
    Dining 41
    Food Service 41
    Food Storage 41
    Sanitation and Hygiene 42
    Housekeeping 42
    Clothing and Supplies 42
    Personal Property 42
    Mechanical Equipment 42
    Commissary/Canteen 42

Contents

Section F
Administrative and Staff Areas
    Administrative Areas 43
    Staff Areas 43
    Accessibility to the Handicapped 43

Section G
Security
    Control Center 44
    Perimeter Security 44
    Entrances and Exits 44
    Security Equipment Storage 44

Part Three
Institutional Operations 3-ALDF-3A-01—3E-11

Section A
Security and Control
    Security Manual 47
    Control Center 47
    Correctional Officer Assignments 47
    Permanent Log 49
    Patrols and Inspections 49
    Inmate Counts 50
    Inmate Movement 50
    Use of Restraints 50
    Control of Contraband 51
    Controlled Access and Use of Keys 52
    Tools and Equipment 52
    Vehicles 52
    Security Equipment 53
    Use of Firearms 54

Section B
Safety and Emergency Procedures
    Fire Safety 55
    Flammable, Toxic, and Caustic Materials 57
    Emergency Power and Communications 57
    Emergency Plans 58
    Evacuation Procedures 59
    Work Stoppage 59
    Threats to Security 60
    Escapes 60

Section C
Rules and Discipline
    Rules of Conduct 61
    Resolution of Minor Infractions 62
    Criminal Violations 62
    Disciplinary Reports 62
    Prehearing Action 63
    Disciplinary Hearing 64
    Conduct of Hearing 64

Hearing Record 65
Review 66
Appeal 66

Section D
Special Management
General Policy and Practice 67
Admission and Review of Status 68
Supervision 69
General Conditions of Confinement 70
Programs and Services 71
Visiting 71
Access to Legal and Reading Materials 71
Exercise Outside of Cell 71
Telephone Privileges 72
Administrative Segregation/Protective Custody 72

Section E
Inmate Rights
Access to Courts 73
Access to Counsel 73
Access to Law Library 73
Access to Programs and Services 74
Access to Media 74
Protection from Harm 74
Protection from Unreasonable Searches 75
Freedom in Personal Grooming 75
Grievance Procedures 75

Part Four 3-ALDF-4A-01—4G-07
Institutional Services

Section A
Reception and Orientation
Personal Property 78

Section B
Classification
Special Management Inmates 79

Section C
Food Service
Food Service Management 80
Budgeting and Purchasing 80
Dietary Allowances 81
Menu Planning 81
Special Diets 81
Health and Safety Regulations 82
Inspections 83
Facilities and Equipment 84
Meal Service 84

Section D
Sanitation and Hygiene

- Sanitation Inspections 85
- Water Supply 85
- Waste Disposal 85
- Housekeeping 86
- Clothing and Bedding Supplies 86
- Clothing Issue 86
- Bedding and Linen Issue 87
- Hair Care Services 87

Section E
Health Care

- General Policies 89
- Unimpeded Access to Care 89
- Facilities and Equipment 89
- Personnel 90
- Administration of Treatment 91
- Mental Health Services 91
- Health-trained Staff Member 91
- Students and Interns 92
- Inmate Assistants 92
- Pharmaceuticals 93
- Health Screenings and Examinations 94
- Dental Screening and Examination 97
- Levels of Care 97
- First Aid 97
- Sick Call 98
- Use of Specialists 98
- Prostheses and Orthodontic Devices 98
- Transfer for Needed Care 99
- Use of Restraints 99
- Specialized Programs 100
- Suicide Prevention and Intervention 100
- Serious and Infectious Diseases 100
- Severe Mental Illness and Retardation 101
- Detoxification 101
- Management of Chemical Dependency 102
- Informed Consent 102
- Inmate Participation in Research 102
- Notification of Designated Individuals 103
- Inmate Death 103
- Health Record Files 103
- Confidentiality 104
- Transferred and Inactive Records 104

Section F
Social Services

- Counseling 105
- Counseling for Pregnant Inmates 105
- Substance Abuse Programs 106

Section G
Release
    Release Preparation 107
    Temporary and Graduated Release 107
    Final Release 108

Part Five
Inmate Programs 3-ALDF-5A-01—5F-10

Section A
Work and Correctional Industries
    Inmate Work Plan 109
    Work Opportunities 110
    Work, Health, and Safety Standards 111
    Correctional Industries 111
    Inmate Compensation 112

Section B
Academic and Vocational Education
    Comprehensive Education Program 113

Section C
Recreation and Activities
    Comprehensive Recreational Program 114
    Equipment and Facilities 114

Section D
Mail, Telephone, and Visiting
    Mail 115
    Access to Publications 115
    Inspection of Letters and Packages 116
    Telephone 117
    Visiting 117
    Extended and Special Visits 117
    Visitor Registration 118

Section E
Library
    Comprehensive Library Services 119
    Selection and Acquisition of Materials 119

Section F
Religious Programs
    Program Coordination and Supervision 120
    Opportunity to Practice One's Faith 121
    Religious Facilities and Equipment 122

Appendices
    Appendix A 123
    Appendix B 125
    Glossary 130
    Index 148

Introduction to Accreditation

The American Correctional Association (ACA) and the Commission on Accreditation for Corrections (CAC) are private, nonprofit organizations that administer the only national accreditation program for all components of adult and juvenile corrections. Their purpose is to promote improvement in the management of correctional agencies through the administration of a voluntary accreditation program and the ongoing development and revision of relevant, useful standards.

Accreditation, a process that began in 1978, involves approximately 80 percent of all state departments of corrections and youth services as active participants. Also included are programs and facilities operated by the Federal Bureau of Prisons, the U.S. Parole Commission, and the District of Columbia.

For these agencies, the accreditation program offers the opportunity to evaluate their operations against national standards, remedy deficiencies, and upgrade the quality of correctional programs and services. The recognized benefits from such a process include improved management, a defense against lawsuits through documentation and the demonstration of a "good faith" effort to improve conditions of confinement, increased accountability and enhanced public credibility for administrative and line staff, a safer and more humane environment for personnel and offenders, and the establishment of measurable criteria for upgrading programs, personnel, and physical plant on a continuing basis.

The timeliness, requirements, and outcomes of the accreditation process are the same for a state or federal prison, training school, local detention facility, private halfway house or group home, probation and parole field service agency, or paroling authority. All programs and facilities sign a contract, pay an accreditation fee, conduct a self-evaluation, and have a Standards Compliance Audit by trained ACA consultants prior to an accreditation decision by the Board of Commissioners. Once accredited, all programs and facilities submit annual certification statements to the ACA. Also, at the ACA's expense and discretion, a monitoring visit may be conducted during the initial three-year accreditation period to ensure continued compliance with the appropriate standards.

Participation in the Accreditation Process

Invitations to participate in the accreditation process have been extended to all adult and juvenile agencies for which standards have been developed and published. Participating agencies include public and private agencies; federal, state, and local agencies; and United States and Canadian correctional agencies.

Accreditation activities are initiated voluntarily by correctional administrators. When an agency elects to pursue accreditation, ACA staff will provide the agency with appropriate information and application materials. These include a contract, the applicable manual of standards, a policy and procedure manual, and an Organization Summary (narrative).

Eligibility Criteria

To be eligible for accreditation, an agency must be part of a governmental entity or conform to the applicable federal, state, and local laws and regulations regarding corporate existence. The agency must (1) hold under confinement pretrial or presentenced adults or juveniles who are being held pending a hearing for unlawful activity; OR (2) hold under confinement sentenced adult offenders convicted of criminal activity or juveniles adjudicated to confinement; OR (3) supervise in the community sentenced adult or adjudicated juvenile offenders, including youth placed in residential settings; and (4) have a single administrative officer responsible for agency operations. It is this administrative officer who makes formal application for admission to accreditation.

It is the ACA's policy that nonadjudicated juveniles should be served outside of the juvenile correctional system. Training schools housing status offenders must remove them before the facility can be awarded accreditation. Detention facilities may house status offenders who have violated valid court orders by continued commission of status offenses. In such instances, the following conditions would apply: status offenders are separated by sight and sound from delinquent offenders; facility staff demonstrate attempts to mandate removal of all status offenders from detention centers; and special programs are developed for status offenders.

The ACA does not prohibit the participation in accreditation of community programs that commingle adjudicated delinquents with status offenders in nonsecure settings. However, the ACA actively supports and requires exclusion of status offenders from the criminal and juvenile justice systems. Residential and institutional programs and facilities that commingle adults and juveniles (separated by sight and sound) may become accredited. Individual cases may stipulate removal of juveniles prior to receiving an accreditation award.

Preaccreditation Assessment

Prior to signing an accreditation contract, an agency may request a preaccreditation assessment. The assessment entails a visit to the agency by an ACA consultant, who will assess strengths and areas for improvement, measure readiness for application for accreditation, and identify steps required to achieve accreditation. A confidential written report is provided for the agency to assist in making the decision to apply for accreditation.

Applicant Status

When the agency enters accreditation, the administrator requests an information package from the ACA. In order to confirm eligibility, determine appropriate fees, and schedule accreditation activities, the agency in turn provides the ACA with relevant narrative information through the Organization Summary.

Both the completed Organization Summary, which provides a written description of the facility/program, and the signed contract must be returned to the ACA for an agency to initiate the accreditation process. The association will notify the agency of its acceptance into the accreditation process within fifteen days of receipt of the necessary application materials. The ACA will then assign a Regional Administrator from the Division of Standards and Accreditation as a permanent liaison to the agency. The agency will appoint an Accreditation Manager, who will be responsible for organizing and supervising agency resources and activities to achieve accreditation.

As delineated in the contract, the fees for the accreditation period cover all services normally provided to an agency by ACA staff, consultants, and the Board of Commissioners. The fees are determined during the application period and are included in the contract signed by the agency and the ACA.

The fees for probation, parole, and aftercare field service agencies depend on the size, number, and locations of the field offices. The central office and a stipulated number of field offices are audited, with the fee determined by the number of consultant days and auditors required to complete the audit.

Correspondent Status

When the application is accepted, the agency enters Correspondent Status. During this time, the agency conducts a self-assessment of its operations and completes a Self-evaluation Report, which specifies the agency's level of standards compliance. (Self-evaluation Reports are optional for facilities signing a reaccreditation contract.)

At the agency's request and expense, an on-site accreditation orientation for staff and/or a field consultation is scheduled. The object of the orientation is to adequately prepare agency staff to complete the requirements of accreditation, including an understanding of self-evaluation activities, compilation of documentation, audit procedures, and standards interpretation. A field consultant provides information on accreditation policy and procedure, standards interpretations, and/or documentation requirements. Agency familiarity with standards and accreditation is the key factor in determining the need for these services.

The Self-evaluation Report includes the Organization Summary, a compliance tally, preliminary requests for Waivers or Plans of Action, and completed Standards Compliance Checklists for each standard in the applicable manual.

Applicable Standards

The standards used for accreditation address services, programs, and operations essential to good correctional management, including administrative and fiscal controls, staff training and development, physical plant, safety and emergency procedures, sanitation, food service, rules and discipline, and a variety of subjects that comprise good correctional practice. These standards are under continual revision to reflect changing practice, current case law, new knowledge, and agency experience with their application. These changes are published by the ACA in the *Standards Supplement*.

ACA policy addresses the impact of the standards revisions on agencies involved in accreditation. Agencies signing contracts after the date that a *Standards Supplement* is published are held accountable for all standards changes in that supplement. Agencies are not held accountable for changes made after the contract is signed. The agencies may elect to apply new changes to the standards that have been issued following the program's

Introduction to Accreditation

entry into accreditation. Agencies must notify the ACA of their decision prior to conducting the Standards Compliance Audit.

Although accreditation is based only on the ACA standards, provision is made for recognition of accreditations earned from the Joint Commission on Accreditation of Hospitals. This covers the accreditation of medical services in local detention facilities and JCAH accreditation of institutional hospital programs.

Relative to the physical plant standards, the edition of the standards that was used in the design, building, and/or renovation of a facility shall be applicable for purposes of accreditation and all reaccreditations. The ACA reserves the right to add physical plant standards for reaccreditation if such standards can be met without major modification to the design and/or building of the facility (e.g., accessibility for handicapped staff and inmates).

For accreditation purposes, any new architectural design, building, and/or renovation of the institution must be in accordance with the edition of the standards current at the time of such design, building, and/or renovation. In such cases, different standards would be applied to separate parts of the institution respective to these changes in the physical plant.

In completing a Standards Compliance Checklist, the agency checks *compliance, noncompliance,* or *not applicable* for each standard. Checking *compliance* means the agency complies completely with the content of the standard at all times and has documentation (primarily written) available to support compliance. A finding of *noncompliance* indicates that all or part of the requirements stated in the standard have not been met. A *not applicable* response means that the standard is clearly not relevant to the situation being audited. A written statement supporting nonapplicability of the standard is required.

At this time, the agency may request a Plan-of-action Waiver for one or more standards, provided that overall agency programming compensates for the lack of compliance. The Waiver request is accompanied by a clear explanation of such compensating conditions. The agency applies for a Waiver only when the totality of conditions safeguards the life, health, and safety of offenders and staff. Waivers are not granted for standards designated as mandatory. Also, the granting of a Waiver does not change the conclusion of noncompliance or the agency's compliance tally. When a Plan-of-action Waiver is requested during the self-evaluation phase, the ACA staff renders a preliminary judgement. A final decision can only be made by the Board of Commissioners during the accreditation hearing. Most Waivers granted are for physical plant standards.

Agencies have the option of submitting the completed Self-evaluation Report to the ACA for review, or they may certify its completion in writing and request placement in Candidate Status. For agencies undergoing accreditation for the first time, it is suggested that the report be reviewed by the ACA staff, primarily to verify agency understanding of accreditation requirements. The documentation that the agency staff has compiled to support its findings of standards compliance remains at the agency, where it will be examined by ACA consultants who conduct the Standards Compliance Audit.

The compilation of written documentation requires the most time and effort during Correspondent Status. A separate documentation file, which explicitly shows compliance, is prepared for each standard.

In order to request an audit, an agency must comply with 100 percent of the standards designated as mandatory and 90 percent of the nonmandatory standards. (The Self-evaluation Report does not necessarily need to reflect these levels of compliance.)

Candidate Status

The agency enters into Candidate Status with ACA's acceptance of the Self-evaluation Report or agency certification of its completion. Candidate Status continues until the agency meets the required level of compliance, has been audited by a Visiting Committee composed of ACA consultants, and has been awarded or denied a three-year accreditation by the Board of Commissioners. Candidate Status lasts up to twelve months.

An agency may request, in writing, an extension of Candidate Status, stating the reasons for the request. The ACA staff considers the request and renders a decision. It is ACA policy that extensions of Candidate Status do not exceed twelve months. Facilities requesting extensions beyond their contract expiration date will be assessed an additional annual fee.

The agency requests a standards compliance audit when the facility administrator believes the agency or facility has met or exceeded the compliance levels required for accreditation (100 percent mandatory; 90 percent nonmandatory).

Standards Compliance Audit

The agency's request for an audit is made six to eight weeks in advance of the desired audit dates. The purpose of the audit is to have the Visiting Committee measure the agency's operation against the standards, based on the documentation provided by the agency.

A Visiting Committee completes the audit and prepares a Visiting Committee Report for submission to the CAC. The ACA designates a Visiting Committee Chairperson to organize and supervise the committee's activities.

Prior to arrival at the audit site, each member of the Visiting Committee reviews the agency's descriptive narrative and any additional information that the ACA may have provided, including pending litigation and court orders submitted by the agency and any inmate correspondence. The Visiting Committee Chairperson makes audit assignments to each consultant. For example, one consultant may audit the administrative, fiscal, and personnel standards, while another audits standards for physical plant, sanitation, and security.

On arrival, the Visiting Committee meets with the administrator, Accreditation Manager, and other appropriate staff to discuss the scope of the audit and the schedule of activities. This exchange of information provides for development of an audit schedule that ensures the least amount of disruption to routine agency operation.

The exact amount of time required to complete the audit depends on agency size, number of applicable standards, additional facilities to be audited, and the accessibility and organization of documentation. To expedite the audit, all documentation should be clearly referenced and located where the Visiting Committee is to work.

The Accreditation Manager's responsibilities include compiling and making accessible to all Visiting Committee members the standards compliance documentation and release-of-information forms for personnel and offender records. Also, staff should be notified beforehand to ensure their availability to discuss specific issues or conduct tours of the facility for the Visiting Committee.

During the audit, the members of the Visiting Committee tour the facility, review documentation prepared for each standard, and interview staff and offenders to make compliance decisions. The Visiting Committee reports its findings on the same Standards Compliance Checklist used by the agency in preparing its Self-evaluation Report. All members of the Visiting Committee review all mandatory standards, all areas of noncompliance and nonapplicability, and all requests for Waivers, with decisions made collectively. (Final decisions on Waivers can only be approved by the CAC at the time of the agency's accreditation hearing.)

Interviewing staff members and offenders is an integral part of the audit. In addition to speaking with those who request an interview with the team, the members of the Visiting Committee select other individuals to interview and issues to discuss. These are voluntary interviews that occur randomly throughout the audit. The confidentiality of those interviewed is ensured.

In addition to auditing standards documentation, consultants will evaluate the quality of life or conditions of confinement. An acceptable quality of life is necessary for an agency to be eligible for accreditation. Factors that the Visiting Committee consider include the adequacy and quality of programs, activities, and services available to inmates and their involvement in turn; occurrences of disturbances, serious incidents, assaults, or violence, including their frequency and methods of dealing with them to ensure staff and inmate safety; and overall physical conditions, including adequacy of living, support, and program space and institutional maintenance related to sanitation, health, and safety.

Prior to leaving the agency at the conclusion of the audit, the Visiting Committee again meets with the administrator, the Accreditation Manager, and any others selected by the administrator to discuss the results of the audit. During this Exit Interview, the Visiting Committee reports the standards compliance tally and all findings of noncompliance and nonapplicability as well as preliminary decisions on Waivers, stating the reasons for each decision.

At the close of the audit, if the Visiting Committee finds that the agency is in noncompliance with one or more mandatory standards or does not meet sufficient nonmandatory standards compliance levels to be considered for accreditation, the chairperson advises the agency that an on-site supplemental audit may be required prior to scheduling an accreditation hearing. The agency is responsible for notifying the ACA when the deficiencies have been corrected and a supplemental audit is desired. The agency bears the cost of the supplemental audit. An ACA consultant, often a member of the original Visiting Committee, returns to the

Introduction to Accreditation

agency to reaudit the appropriate standards. The Visiting Committee Report includes the written report from the supplemental audit.

The chairperson of the Visiting Committee prepares and submits a copy of the Visiting Committee Report to the ACA staff within ten days of the completion of the audit. ACA staff review the report for completeness, enter the data, and, within fifteen days of the audit's completion, submit it to the agency administrator and other members of the Visiting Committee for concurrence. On receipt of the Visiting Committee Report, the agency has fifteen days to submit to the ACA staff and all members of the Visiting Committee its written response to the report.

The Accreditation Hearing

The CAC Board of Commissioners is solely responsible for rendering accreditation decisions and is divided into Accreditation Panels empowered to render such decisions. Panels meet separately or in conjunction with a full board meeting and are composed of three to five commissioners.

The agency is invited, at its own expense, to have representation at the accreditation hearing. Unless circumstances dictate otherwise, a member of the Visiting Committee is not present; however, an ACA staff member does participate. At the accreditation hearing, the agency representative provides information about the agency, speaks in support of its Appeals and/or Waiver requests, and addresses concerns the panel may have regarding the accreditation application.

After completing its review, an Accreditation Panel votes to award or deny accreditation or continue the agency in Candidate Status. If, in the opinion of the panel members, the circumstances merit such action, the panel may request full board consideration of an accreditation decision.

When an agency receives a three-year accreditation award, a certificate with the effective date of the award is presented to the agency representative. The Board of Commissioners may request additional tasks from the agency prior to granting an accreditation award, such as submission of acceptable Plans of Action or a monitoring visit. These requests are specific as to activities required and timeliness for their completion. The panel advises the agency representative of all changes at the time the accreditation decision is made.

The ACA and the CAC may deny accreditation for reasons of insufficient standards compliance, inadequate Plans of Action, or failure to meet other requirements as determined by the Board of Commissioners, including, but not limited to, the conditions of confinement in a given facility. It is the position of the ACA that it may stipulate additional requirements for accreditation if, in its opinion, conditions exist in the facility or program that adversely affect the life, health, or safety of the staff or offenders.

In not awarding accreditation, the CAC may extend an agency in Candidate Status for a specified period of time and for identified deficiencies if, in its judgement, the agency is actively pursuing compliance. Those agencies denied accreditation but not extended in Candidate Status may reapply for accreditation after 180 days. The agency receives written notification of all decisions relative to its accreditation following the accreditation hearing.

Accredited Status

During the three-year accreditation period, the ACA requires that accredited agencies submit annual certification statements confirming continued standards compliance at levels necessary for accreditation. The report should be inclusive of the agency's progress on completing Plans of Action and other significant events that may affect the accreditation award. In addition, the ACA may require accredited agencies to submit written responses to public criticism, notoriety, or patterns of complaints about agency activity that suggest a failure to maintain standards compliance. The ACA, at its own expense and with advance notice, may conduct on-site monitoring visits to verify continued standards compliance or conditions of confinement.

Reconsideration Process

The goal of the ACA's accreditation process is to ensure the equity, fairness, and reliability of its decisions, particularly those that constitute either denial or revocation of Accredited Status. Therefore, an agency may request reconsideration of any denial or revocation of accreditation. However, the reasonableness of the ACA's standards, criteria, and/or procedures for accreditation may not serve as the basis for reconsideration.

A reconsideration request is based on the grounds that the adverse decision is (1) arbitrary, capricious, or otherwise in substantial disregard of the criteria and/or procedures for accreditation as promulgated by the

ACA, (2) based on incorrect facts or an incorrect interpretation of facts, or (3) unsupported by substantial evidence.

The agency submits a written request for reconsideration to the ACA staff within thirty days of the adverse decision, stating the basis for the request. The CAC's Executive Committee reviews the request and decides whether there is sufficient evidence to warrant a reconsideration hearing before the Board of Commissioners. The agency is notified in writing of the Executive Committee's decision.

Revocation of Accreditation

An accredited agency that does not maintain the required levels of compliance throughout the three-year accreditation period, including continuous compliance with all mandatory standards, may have its accreditation award revoked. The agency is notified of its deficiencies and given a specified amount of time to correct them. If the deficiencies continue, the Board of Commissioners may place the agency on Probationary Status for an additional stated period of time, requiring documentation of compliance. Should the agency fail to correct the deficiencies, the Board of Commissioners may revoke the agency's accreditation and request that the Accreditation Certificate be returned to the ACA.

An accredited agency that has had its accreditation revoked for reasons of noncompliance also may use the reconsideration process.

Reaccreditation

To ensure continuous Accredited Status, accredited agencies should apply for reaccreditation approximately twelve months prior to the expiration of their current accreditation award. Agencies have the option of being audited from individual accreditation files or operational files. For detailed information on reaccreditation, consult your ACA Regional Administrator.

The preceding information is provided as an overview of the accreditation process. Additional information on specific procedures and elements of the process is available from the ACA Division of Standards and Accreditation.

Part One
Administration and Management

Section A
General Administration

Principle: A written body of policy and procedure establishes the facility's goals, objectives, and standard operating procedures and establishes a system of regular review.

Purpose and Mission

3-ALDF-1A-01
(Ref. 2-5001)

There is a statute authorizing the establishment of the local detention facility or its parent agency.

Comment:
None.

3-ALDF-1A-02
(Ref. 2-5001)

There is a written document delineating the agency's mission. This document is reviewed at least annually and updated as needed.

Comment:
The mission statement should address programs and services that are available in the facility. Programs include receiving and diagnostic units, prerelease units, separate units for special offenders, etc.

Policy and Goal Formulation

3-ALDF-1A-03
(Ref. 2-5003)

Written policy, procedure, and practice provide that the facility administrator formulates goals for the facility at least annually and translates them into measurable objectives.

Comment:
Goals facilitate decision making, especially in an atmosphere of change. Measurable objectives facilitate the process of program review, monitoring, and evaluation.

3-ALDF-1A-04
(Ref. 2-5004)

Written policy, procedure, and practice provide that employees participate in the formulation of policies, procedures, and programs.

Comment:
Employee participation can be achieved through staff meetings, suggestion programs, employee councils, and similar formats.

3-ALDF-1A-05
(Ref. 2-5005)

Written policy, procedure, and practice demonstrate that related community agencies with which the facility has contact participate in policy development, coordinated planning, and interagency consultation.

Comment:
The conduct of the facility affects and is affected by agencies and groups within and outside the criminal justice system. Interaction with these organizations creates a forum for coordination and cooperation.

Appointed Personnel

Warden/Superintendent

3-ALDF-1A-06
(Ref. 2-5006)

Written policy, procedure, and practice provide that the facility is managed by a single administrator to whom all employees or units of management are responsible.

Comment:
None.

3-ALDF-1A-07
(Ref. 2-5007)

When the facility administrator position is filled by appointment, the facility administrator is appointed by the chief executive officer or governing board of the parent agency.

Comment:
None.

Qualifications

3-ALDF-1A-08
(Ref. 2-5008)

The qualifications, authority, and responsibilities of the facility administrator and other appointed personnel who are not covered by merit systems, civil service regulation, or union contract are specified in writing by statute or by the parent agency.

Comment:
Explicit position descriptions for facility appointments ensure that personnel meet minimum standards and reduce opportunities for political interference in appointments.

3-ALDF-1A-09
(Ref. 2-5009)

The qualifications for the position of facility administrator include at a minimum the following: a bachelor's degree in an appropriate discipline; five years of related administrative experience; and demonstrated administrative ability and leadership. The degree requirement may be satisfied by completion of a career development program that includes work-related experience, training, or college credits at a level of achievement equivalent to the bachelor's degree.

Comment:
Establishing high qualifications ensures that only qualified individuals are recruited and hired. It is the agency's responsibility to see that potential administrators receive the required education.

Term of Office

3-ALDF-1A-10
(Ref. 2-5010)

Written policy, procedure, and practice provide that the term of the facility administrator is continuous, except for assignment to a position of equal responsibility, and may be terminated by the appointing authority and, if requested, subsequent to a formal hearing.

Comment:
Tenure for the facility administrator helps ensure a high-quality operation. Many of these positions are no longer covered by civil service provisions. In these cases, the appointing authority should make it clear that the tenure is continuous within the system and that removal from office follows a prescribed and fair process.

Table of Organization

3-ALDF-1A-11
(Ref. 2-5012)

There is a written document describing the facility's organization. The description includes an organizational chart that groups similar functions, services, and activities in administrative subunits. This document is reviewed annually and updated as needed.

Comment:
A current organizational chart is necessary for providing a clear administrative picture. The chart should reflect the grouping of functions, the effective span of control, lines of authority, and orderly channels of communication.

3-ALDF-1A-12
(Ref. 2-5011)

Written policy and procedure, which are reviewed annually, specify the roles and functions of employees of other agencies providing a service to the facility.

Comment:
None.

Policy and Procedure Manuals

3-ALDF-1A-13
(Ref. 2-5015)

The policies and procedures for operating and maintaining the facility and its satellites are specified in a manual that is accessible to all employees and the public. This manual is reviewed at least annually and updated as needed.

Comment:
A government agency has an obligation to make public its philosophy, goals, and objectives. A program should be conducted to familiarize employees with the manual.

Part One. Administration and Management

3-ALDF-1A-14
(Ref. 2-5015)

Each department and major administrative unit in the facility maintains and makes available to employees a manual of standard operating procedures that specifies how policies are to be implemented. These procedures are reviewed at least annually and are updated as needed.

Comment:
Detailed manuals of standard operating procedures assist employees in successfully carrying out their assignments and help ensure overall conformance to facility policy and procedure. All employees should be thoroughly familiar with the sections concerning their particular assignments.

3-ALDF-1A-15
(Ref. 2-5016)

Written policy, procedure, and practice provide that new or revised policies and procedures are disseminated to designated staff and volunteers and, when appropriate, to inmates prior to implementation.

Comment:
Rapid dissemination of policies and procedures increases the effectiveness of the facility's communication system.

Channels of Communication

3-ALDF-1A-16
(Ref. 2-5013)

Written policy, procedure, and practice provide for regular meetings between the facility administrator and all department heads and between department heads and their key staff members. Such meetings are to be conducted at least monthly. There is formal documentation that the meetings are held at least monthly.

Comment:
Regular channels of communication are necessary for delegating authority, assigning responsibility, supervising work, and coordinating efforts.

Monitoring and Assessment

3-ALDF-1A-17
(Ref. 2-5017)

Written policy, procedure, and practice provide operations and programs that are monitored through inspections and reviews. This internal administrative audit should be separate from any external or continuous inspection conducted by other agencies.

Comment:
Timely and periodic assessment can reveal how well a facility's operations and programs are complying with policy and procedure. This internal administrative audit should be separate from any external or continuous inspection conducted by other agencies.

Section A. General Administration

3-ALDF-1A-18
(Ref. 2-5018)

Written policy, procedure, and practice demonstrate that the facility reports its activities at least quarterly to the parent agency. These reports are in writing and include major developments in each department or administrative unit; major incidents; population data; assessment of staff and inmate morale; and major problems and plans for solving them.

Comment:
Routine reporting by individual facilities enables the parent agency to stay informed about programs, activities, and problems throughout the jail. The exchange of reports among facilities offers opportunities for solving problems jointly.

Media Access

3-ALDF-1A-19
(Ref. 2-5023)

Written policy, procedure, and practice grant representatives of the media access to the facility consistent with preserving inmates' right to privacy and maintaining order and security.

Comment:
None.

Legal Counsel

3-ALDF-1A-20
(Ref. 2-5019)

Written policy and procedure specify the circumstances and methods for the facility administrator and other staff to obtain legal assistance as needed in the performance of their duties.

Comment:
Qualified legal assistance is necessary to ensure that policies and procedures are consistent with relevant court decisions. Legal counsel can also advise on meeting statutory and court requirements and on facility operations and individual cases, and provide representation before courts and other bodies. Counsel should be available promptly and continuously.

Political Practices

3-ALDF-1A-21
(Ref. New)

There is a written policy regarding campaigning, lobbying, and political practices. This policy conforms to governmental statutes and regulations and is known and available to all employees.

Comment:
None.

3-ALDF-1A-22
(Ref. New)

There is a population projection plan designed to anticipate the future needs of the facility/agency.

Comment:
There is a need to anticipate and plan for the expected increase or decrease in facility population. The projections should extend for at least five years into the future.

3-ALDF-1A-23
(Ref. New)

There is a contingency plan to provide for the projected population trend. At a minimum, this plan should include staffing requirements, physical plant needs, and budget projections.

Comment:
The specificity of the plan will depend on the complexity of the facility and may range from short, general observations to lengthy scientific research documents.

Section B
Fiscal Management

Principle: A written body of policy and procedure establishes the facility's fiscal planning, budgeting, and accounting procedures and establishes a system of regular review.

Fiscal Control

3-ALDF-1B-01
(Ref. 2-5027)

Consistent with policy, the facility administrator is responsible for fiscal policy, management, and control. Facility staff participate in the preparation of the written budget request. Management of fiscal operations may be delegated to a designated staff person.

Comment:
None.

3-ALDF-1B-02
(Ref. 2-5036)

Written policy, procedure, and practice cover at a minimum the following fiscal areas: internal controls; petty cash; bonding for all appropriate staff; signature control on checks; and the issuing or use of vouchers and methods for writing budgets.

Comment:
None.

3-ALDF-1B-03
(Ref. 2-5029)

The facility administrator participates in budget deliberations conducted by the parent agency or the next higher level of government. This participation includes requests for funds for maintaining the facility's daily operations; financing capital projects; and supporting long-range objectives, program development, and additional staff requirements.

Comment:
None.

Accounting Procedures

3-ALDF-1B-04
(Ref. 2-5034)

Written policy, procedure, and practice demonstrate that the procedures for the collection, safeguarding, and disbursement of monies comply with the accounting procedures established by the governing jurisdiction. These procedures are reviewed annually and updated as needed.

Comment:
The facility's fiscal policies and procedures should be patterned after those of the governing authority and should be compatible with the state's central accounting system. These include policies and procedures for fiscal recordkeeping, reports, reviews, audits, disbursements, position allocations, payroll, cash transactions, commissary/canteen operation, and inmates' personal funds, if any.

3-ALDF-1B-05
(Ref. 2-5033)

The facility's accounting system is designed to show the current status of appropriations and expenditures.

Comment:
Current information is needed to meet objectives, prevent budget discrepancies, respond to emerging needs, and ensure that the flow of funds is proceeding as planned.

Cash Management

3-ALDF-1B-06
(Ref. 2-5035)

Written policy, procedure, and practice provide that all monies collected at the facility are placed in an officially designated and secure location(s) daily.

Comment:
There are safeguards to ensure security in each facility.

3-ALDF-1B-07
(Ref. 2-5038)

The facility administrator, as frequently as required by statute and regulation, prepares and distributes to its parent agency and other designated authorities reports that include, at a minimum, income and expenditures statements, funding source financial reports, and audit reports.

Comment:
None.

Internal Monitoring

3-ALDF-1B-08
(Ref. 2-5038)

Written policy, procedure, and practice provide for ongoing monitoring of the facility's fiscal activities. The results are reported in writing at least quarterly and are forwarded to the parent agency.

Comment:
Internal monitoring allows a facility to determine whether internal control procedures are being followed and to strengthen them where needed.

Independent Audit

3-ALDF-1B-09
(Ref. 2-5037)

Written policy, procedure, and practice provide for an independent financial audit of the facility. This audit is conducted annually or as stipulated by statute or regulation.

Comment:
An outside certified auditing firm or the appropriate governmental auditing team should conduct the audit.

Inventory

3-ALDF-1B-10
(Ref. 2-5039)

Written policy and procedure govern inventory control of property, supplies, and other assets. Inventories are conducted at time periods stipulated by applicable statutes but at least every two years.

Comment:
None.

Section B. Fiscal Management

Purchasing

Supplies and Equipment

3-ALDF-1B-11
(Ref. 2-5040)
Written policy and procedure govern the requisition and purchase of supplies and equipment, including at a minimum the purchasing procedures and criteria for the selection of bidders and vendors.

Comment:
None.

3-ALDF-1B-12
(Ref. 2-5043)
Written policy, procedure, and practice specify that the administrator reviews space and equipment requirements at least annually, reports deficiencies to the parent agency, and plans with the parent agency for the effective use of space and equipment.

Comment:
None.

Community Services

3-ALDF-1B-13
(Ref. New)
Funds are available for purchasing community services to supplement existing programs and services.

Comment:
None.

Position Control

3-ALDF-1B-14
(Ref. 2-5041, 2-5044)
Written policy and procedure regulate position control regarding position allocation, budget authorization, personnel records, and payroll. Information on the number and type of positions filled and vacant should be available at all times. The fiscal office should verify that all payroll positions are authorized in the budget, that all persons on the payroll are legally employed, that attendance records support the payroll, and that needed funds are available. The payroll should be based on timekeeping records.

Comment:
None.

Institutional Insurance

3-ALDF-1B-15
(Ref. 2-5042)
Written policy, procedure, and practice provide for facility insurance coverage, including at a minimum the following: worker's compensation, civil liability for employees, liability for official vehicles, and public employee blanket bond.

Comment:
Coverage can be provided by private companies, a self-insurer's program, or state indemnification.

Part One. Administration and Management

Commissary/Canteen

3-ALDF-1B-16
(Ref. 2-5046)

An inmate commissary or canteen is available where inmates can purchase approved items that are not furnished by the facility. The commissary/canteen's operations are strictly controlled using standard accounting procedures.

Comment:
To minimize differences in individual spending power, restrictions should be placed on purchases, and means of purchase other than cash should be considered.

3-ALDF-1B-17
(Ref. New)

Commissary/canteen funds are audited independently following standard accounting procedures, and an annual financial status report is available as a public document.

Comment:
An annual report outlining the commissary/canteen's financial status helps to safeguard the integrity of these operations.

Inmate Funds

3-ALDF-1B-18
(Ref. 2-5046)

Written policy and procedure govern the operation of any fund established for inmates. Any interest earned on monies other than operating funds accrues to the benefit of the inmates.

Comment:
When money is available from donations, commissary/canteen profits, or other sources, a fund should be established for the benefit of the inmates. The responsibility for administering such a fund should be fixed, and specific guidelines and controls should be established for collecting, safeguarding, and spending these monies. This includes government bonds.

3-ALDF-1B-19
(Ref. New)

Inmates' personal funds held by the facility are controlled by accepted accounting procedures.

Comment:
The responsibility for the control and accounting of inmates' personal funds usually is delegated to the facility's business manager. Inmates should receive receipts for all financial transactions.

3-ALDF-1B-20
(Ref. New)

Written policy, procedure, and practice provide that any financial transactions permitted between inmates must be approved by staff.

Comment:
Uncontrolled financial transactions between inmates can foster illegal activities.

Section C
Personnel

Principle: A written body of policy and procedure establishes the facility's staffing, recruiting, promotion, benefits, and review procedures for employees.

Personnel Policy Manual

3-ALDF-1C-01
(Ref. 2-5063)

A personnel policy manual is available for employee reference and covers at a minimum the following areas:

- organization chart (table of organization)
- recruitment and promotion, including equal employment opportunity provisions
- job descriptions and qualifications, including salary determinations and physical fitness policy
- benefits, holidays, leave, and work hours
- personnel records and employee evaluation
- staff development, including in-service training
- retirement, resignation, and termination
- employee-management relations, including disciplinary procedures and grievance and appeals procedures
- statutes relating to political activities
- insurance/professional liability requirements

New staff are informed in writing of the facility's hostage policy in regard to staff roles and safety.

Comment:
Written personnel regulations help ensure equitable and consistent treatment of all employees. Every employee should have the opportunity to review the personnel manual at the time of employment and thereafter, and employees should be encouraged to ask questions about personnel policies.

3-ALDF-1C-02
(Ref. 2-5061)

The facility administrator reviews the facility's internal personnel policies annually and submits recommended changes to the parent agency.

Comment:
None.

Staffing Requirements

3-ALDF-1C-03 The staffing requirements for all categories of personnel are determined on an ongoing basis to ensure that inmates have access to staff, programs, and services. Staffing requirements should be determined on more than inmate population figures and should include review of staffing needs for health care, academic, vocational, library, recreation, and religious programs and services. Workload ratios should reflect such factors as goals, legal requirements, character and needs of the inmates supervised, and other duties required of staff. Workloads should be sufficiently low to provide access to staff and effective services.

Comment:
None.

3-ALDF-1C-04
(Ref. 2-5068) Written policy and procedure provide for the transfer, assignment and selection of employees on the basis of facility need and the ability of the employee to perform the job.

Comment:
None.

3-ALDF-1C-05
(Ref. 2-5070) The facility uses a formula to determine the number of staff needed for essential positions. The formula considers at a minimum holidays, regular days off, annual leave, and average sick leave.

Comment:
Additional factors that can be included in the formula are time off for training, military leave time, and factors specific to the facility and jurisdiction. Positions requiring staffing for more than one shift and/or more than five days per week should be budgeted for the full staffing needed.

3-ALDF-1C-06
(Ref. 2-5072) The facility administrator can document that the overall vacancy rate among the staff positions authorized for working directly with inmates does not exceed 10 percent for any 18-month period.

Comment:
None.

Section C. Personnel

Equal Employment Opportunity

3-ALDF-1C-07
(Ref. 2-5049)

Written policy specifies that equal employment opportunities exist for all positions. When deficiencies exist regarding the employment of minority groups and women, the facility can document the implementation of an affirmative action program that is approved by the appropriate government agency and can document annual reviews and the changes needed to keep the program current. The affirmative action program also includes corrective actions, when needed, in policies regarding pay rate, demotion, transfer, layoff, termination, and upgrading.

Comment:
None.

Selection and Promotion

3-ALDF-1C-08
(Ref. 2-5047)

Written policy and procedure provide for the selection, retention, and promotion of all personnel on the basis of merit and specified qualifications.

Comment:
None.

3-ALDF-1C-09
(Ref. 2-5066)

Employees on permanent status are terminated or demoted only for just cause and after grievance and appeals procedures, if requested, have been exhausted.

Comment:
None.

Probationary Term

3-ALDF-1C-10
(Ref. 2-5055)

Written policy and procedure provide that employees are appointed initially for a probationary term of not less than six months or more than one year.

Comment:
Employee performance during the probationary period should be evaluated at least every two months, and the employee should be given the opportunity to discuss the evaluation. Forms for evaluation of employee performance should be developed and used. Persons not performing satisfactorily should be terminated during the probationary period.

Provisional Appointments

3-ALDF-1C-11
(Ref. 2-5071)

Written policy, procedure, and practice provide for provisional appointments to ensure that short-term personnel, both full-time and part-time, can be available during emergencies.

Comment:
Civil service, merit system, and union requirements should be modified to allow the short-term employment of additional personnel during vacations, rises in the inmate population, or other situations that leave the facility understaffed. While provisional personnel should meet the minimum requirements for the positions they fill, they should not be considered permanent replacements for permanent personnel.

Criminal Record Check

3-ALDF-1C-12
(Ref. 2-5052)
A criminal record check is conducted on all new employees in accordance with state and federal statutes. The purpose of the check is to detect any criminal convictions that relate specifically to job performance.

Comment:
The facility administrators should know of any criminal conviction that could directly affect an employee's job performance in a facility setting.

Physical Examination

3-ALDF-1C-13
(Ref. 2-5053)
Written policy, procedure, and practice provide that employees who have direct contact with inmates receive a physical examination prior to job assignment. All other employees receive a medical screening prior to job assignment. Employees receive reexaminations according to a defined need or schedule.

Comment:
Staff whose responsibilities include security and control or regular direct contact with inmates must have physical examinations to protect their health and ensure that they can carry out their assignments effectively. The basic health status of all employees should be evaluated against the specific requirements of their assignments. Physical examination and screening procedures may be established by the appropriate medical authority in accordance with applicable laws and regulations.

3-ALDF-1C-14
(Ref. 2-5054)
Written policy and procedure promote the physical fitness of staff.

Comment:
None.

Drug-free Workplace

3-ALDF-1C-15
(Ref. 2-5053-1)
There is a written policy and procedure that specifies support for a drug-free workplace for all employees. This policy, which is reviewed at least annually, includes at a minimum the following:

- prohibition of the use of illegal drugs
- prohibition of possession of any illegal drug except in the performance of official duties
- the procedures to be used to ensure compliance
- the opportunities available for treatment and/or counseling for drug abuse
- the penalties for violation of the policy

Comment:
None.

Section C. Personnel

Performance Reviews

3-ALDF-1C-16
(Ref. 2-5067)

Written policy, procedure, and practice provide for an annual written performance review of each employee. The review is based on defined criteria, and the results are discussed with the employee.

Comment:
Performance review should be an ongoing process with written evaluations completed at least annually. Reviews should be objective and based on specific job criteria and explicit performance standards.

Compensation and Benefits

3-ALDF-1C-17
(Ref. 2-5057)

Compensation and benefit levels for all facility personnel are comparable to those for similar occupational groups in the state or region.

Comment:
Competitive salaries and attractive benefits are necessary to recruit and retain staff of high caliber. Occupational fields with positions similar to those in the correctional field include education, social work, accounting, and office management.

3-ALDF-1C-18
(Ref. 2-5058)

Compensation and benefits for correctional officers are at least equal to those for law enforcement officers working in the same organization.

Comment:
None.

3-ALDF-1C-19
(Ref. 2-5056)

A written compensation and benefit plan exists. Employees have access to information on compensation and benefits and receive this information during new employee orientation.

Comment:
None.

3-ALDF-1C-20
(Ref. 2-5059)

Written policy, procedure, and practice provide for employees to be reimbursed for all approved expenses incurred in the performance of their duties.

Comment:
Funds should be available for approved reimbursements.

Personnel Files

3-ALDF-1C-21
(Ref. 2-5073)

The facility maintains a current, accurate, confidential personnel record on each employee.

Comment:
The personnel record should contain the following: initial application; reference letters; results of employment investigation; verification of training and experience; wage and salary information; medical evaluations; job performance evaluations; incident reports, if any; and commendations and disciplinary actions, if any.

3-ALDF-1C-22
(Ref. 2-5075)

Written policy, procedure, and practice provide that employees may challenge the information in their personnel file and have it corrected or removed if it is proved inaccurate.

Comment:
Employees should be allowed to review their personnel files to see that they are current and to check for omissions or inaccuracies. Procedures should specify the means for correcting discrepancies.

Code of Ethics

3-ALDF-1C-23
(Ref. 2-5064)

A written code of ethics that prohibits employees from using their official position to secure privileges for themselves or others and from engaging in activities that constitute a conflict of interest is provided to all employees.

Comment:
To protect the integrity of the facility, its staff, and the parent agency, all personnel must be thoroughly familiar with the code of ethics, and the code must be strictly enforced.

Confidentiality of Information

3-ALDF-1C-24
(Ref. 2-5065)

Written policy, procedure, and practice provide that consultants and contract personnel who work with inmates are informed in writing about the facility's policies on confidentiality of information and agree to abide by them.

Comment:
The written policies should specify what types of information are confidential between worker and inmate, what types should be shared with other facility personnel, and what types can be communicated to persons outside the facility.

Employee Assistance Program

3-ALDF-1C-25
(Ref. 2-5075-1)

Written policy, procedure, and practice provide for an employee assistance program that is approved by the parent agency.

Comment:
An employee assistance program provides counseling and/or referral to any employee with a personal problem that is affecting or has the potential to affect the individual's work performance. The program assists the employee in identifying the problem and locating sources of treatment or rehabilitative help.

Section D
Training and Staff Development

Principle: A written body of policy and procedure establishes the facility's training and staff development programs, including training requirements for all categories of personnel.

3-ALDF-1D-01
(Ref. 2-5076)
Written policy, procedure, and practice provide that the facility's employee staff development and training programs are planned, coordinated, and supervised by a qualified employee. The training plan is reviewed annually.

Comment:
The training plan should include all preservice, in-service, and specialized training curriculums, with specific timelines for completing each training unit. The plan should consider the facility's mission, physical characteristics, and specific inmate populations.

Training

3-ALDF-1D-02
(Ref. 2-5078-1)
The facility's training plan provides for ongoing formal evaluation of all preservice, in-service, and specialized training programs. A written report is prepared annually.

Comment:
Ongoing evaluation should include appraisals from trainees, supervisors, and inmates.

Training Resources

Reference Services

3-ALDF-1D-03
(Ref. 2-5079)
Library and reference services are available to complement the training and staff development program.

Comment:
Reference materials should be readily accessible to employees. Materials not usually available at the facility should be acquired through other sources, such as criminal justice clearinghouses and interlibrary loans.

Outside Resources

3-ALDF-1D-04
(Ref. 2-5079)
Written policy, procedure, and practice provide that the training and staff development program uses outside resources when appropriate.

Comment:
Outside guidance and assistance for the facility's training program can take the form of materials, equipment, course development, and evaluation techniques. Numerous resources exist, including the National Institute of Corrections and its National Academy of Corrections, the National Institute of Justice, large corporations, and professional groups.

Part One. Administration and Management

3-ALDF-1D-05 Written policy and procedure provide for collaboration with colleges and univer-
(Ref. 2-5022) sities in areas of mutual interest, when such resources are available.

Comment:
None.

Training Plan

3-ALDF-1D-06 The training plan is developed, evaluated, and updated based on an annual
(Ref. 2-5081-1) assessment that identifies current job-related training needs.

Comment:
Training should be responsive to position requirements, professional development needs, current correctional issues, and new theories, techniques, and technologies. The annual needs assessment may require information from many sources: observation and analysis of job components; staff surveys regarding training needs; reviews of agency/facility operations; staff reports; and evaluations and findings from sources within and outside the jurisdiction.

3-ALDF-1D-07 The facility's training plan is developed by an advisory training committee
(Ref. 2-5078) composed of the facility's training coordinator and representatives from other
facility departments. The committee meets at least quarterly to review progress
and resolve problems, and a written record of these meetings is forwarded to the
warden/superintendent.

Comment:
None.

Space and Equipment

3-ALDF-1D-08 The necessary space and equipment for the training and staff development
(Ref. New) program are available.

Comment:
None.

Reimbursement

3-ALDF-1D-09 The facility budget includes funds to reimburse staff for additional time spent in
(Ref. 2-5080) training or for replacement personnel required when regular personnel are off
duty for training purposes.

Comment:
None.

3-ALDF-1D-10 The facility administration encourages employees to continue their education and
(Ref. 2-5089) provides reimbursement to employees attending approved professional meetings,
seminars, and similar work-related activities.

Comment:
None.

Section D. Training and Staff Development

Training Requirements

Orientation

3-ALDF-1D-11
(Ref. 2-5081)

Written policy and procedure provide that all new clerical/support employees who have minimal inmate contact receive 16 hours of orientation and training during their first year of employment. All persons in this category are given an additional 16 hours of training each subsequent year of employment.

Comment:
None.

3-ALDF-1D-12
(Ref. 2-5083)

Written policy, procedure, and practice provide that all new correctional officers receive 40 hours of training prior to entry on duty, an additional 120 hours of training during their first year of employment, and an additional 40 hours of training each subsequent year of employment. At a minimum, this training covers the following areas:

- security procedures
- supervision of inmates
- signs of suicide risk
- suicide precautions
- use-of-force regulations and tactics
- report writing
- inmate rules and regulations
- rights and responsibilities of inmates
- fire and emergency procedures
- firearms training
- key control
- interpersonal relations
- social/cultural lifestyles of the inmate population
- communication skills
- first aid
- cardiopulmonary resuscitation (CPR)

Comment:
Since the duties of correctional officers frequently involve most facility operations, their training should be comprehensive. Ongoing training during subsequent years of employment enables employees to sharpen skills and keep abreast of changes in operational procedures.

Administrative Staff

3-ALDF-1D-13
(Ref. 2-5084)

Written policy, procedure, and practice provide that all administrative and managerial staff receive 40 hours of training in addition to orientation training during their first year of employment and 40 hours of training each year thereafter. This training covers at a minimum the following areas:

- general management
- labor law
- employee-management relations
- the criminal justice system
- relationships with other service agencies

Comment:
None.

Support Staff

3-ALDF-1D-14
(Ref. 2-5082)

Written policy, procedure, and practice provide that all support employees who have regular or daily contact with inmates receive 40 hours of training in addition to orientation training during their first year of employment and 40 hours of training each year thereafter.

Comment:
Food service employees, industry supervisors, and other support personnel whose work requires day-to-day contact with inmates should receive basic training in inmate supervision and security as well as specialized training in their field as it relates to the facility setting.

Part-time Staff

3-ALDF-1D-15
(Ref. 2-5086)

All part-time staff and contract personnel receive formal orientation appropriate to their assignments and additional training as needed.

Comment:
Part-time staff should receive orientation to facility rules, security, and operational procedures.

Specialized Training

Emergency Unit

3-ALDF-1D-16
(Ref. 2-5085)

Written policy, procedure, and practice provide that correctional officers assigned to an emergency unit have at least one year of experience as a correctional officer and 40 hours of specialized training before undertaking their assignments. The specialized training may be part of the officer's first-year training program. Officers on emergency units receive 40 hours of training annually, at least 16 of which are specifically related to emergency unit assignment.

Comment:
None.

Section D. Training and Staff Development

Use of Force

3-ALDF-1D-17
(Ref. 2-5088)

All security and custody personnel are trained in approved methods of self-defense and the use of force as a last resort to control inmates.

Comment:
All security and custody personnel should be trained in the techniques of using physical force to control and/or move inmates with minimal harm and discomfort to both inmates and staff.

Use of Firearms

3-ALDF-1D-18
(Ref. 2-5087)
Mandatory

Written policy, procedure, and practice provide that all personnel authorized to use firearms receive appropriate training before being assigned to a post involving the possible use of such weapons. Firearms training covers the use, safety, and care of firearms and the constraints on their use. All personnel authorized to use firearms must demonstrate competency in their use at least annually.

Comment:
Firearms training should be thorough, documented, and conducted using a systematic curriculum.

Use of Chemical Agents

3-ALDF-1D-19
(Ref. 2-5087)
Mandatory

All personnel authorized to use chemical agents receive thorough training in their use and in the treatment of individuals exposed to a chemical agent.

Comment:
A special training curriculum should be established that includes both individual and group instruction by competent authorities.

Continuing Education

3-ALDF-1D-20
(Ref. 2-5089)

Written policy, procedure, and practice encourage employees to continue their education.

Comment:
Employees who wish to continue their education should be given the opportunity to do so. Every effort should be made to coordinate educational activities with staff responsibilities. The facility's staff development and training program should promote and support employee participation in outside workshops, seminars, and other formal educational programs.

3-ALDF-1D-21
(Ref. 2-5089)

The facility encourages and provides administrative leave and/or reimbursement for employees attending approved professional meetings, seminars, and similar work-related activities.

Comment:
The facility should encourage participation in outside training and educational programs, including membership in local, state, and national professional organizations. Adequate funds for this purpose should be included in the budget.

3-ALDF-1D-22 Written policy, procedure, and practice provide that on-the-job training is provided to enhance the performance of all full-time employees during their probationary period.
(Ref. New)

Comment:
On-the-job training provided by experienced staff personnel can be a very important vehicle for the transfer of information.

Section E
Case Records

Principle: A written body of policy and procedure establishes the facility's management of case records, including security, right of access, and release of information.

Case Record Management

3-ALDF-1E-01
(Ref. 2-5100)
Written policy and procedure govern case record management, including at a minimum the following areas: the establishment, use, and content of inmate records; right to privacy; secure placement and preservation of records; and schedule for retiring or destroying inactive records. The record and procedures are reviewed annually.

Comment:
An orderly and timely system for recording, maintaining, and using data about offenders increases the efficiency and effectiveness of program and service delivery and the transfer of information to the courts and release authorities.

Transfer of Records

3-ALDF-1E-02
(Ref. New)
Written policy, procedure, and practice provide that an updated case file for any inmate transferred from one facility to another is transferred simultaneously or, at the latest, within 72 hours,

Comment:
Continuity of correctional programming for inmates transferred from other facilities requires that staff have the benefit of a complete cumulative case record as soon as possible. The same policy and procedure should apply to the transfer of medical files.

Computation of Time Served

3-ALDF-1E-03
(Ref. New)
Written policy, procedure, and practice provide that inmate time is accurately computed and recorded in conformance with applicable statutes and regulations.

Comment:
The accurate computation and recording of any "good time" earned or time forfeited is vital for incarcerated persons. Each inmate's case file should include an up-to-date record of time served and time remaining.

Inmate Access to Records

3-ALDF-1E-04
(Ref. 2-5105)
Written policy and procedure govern inmates' access to information in their case records.

Comment:
Inmates should have access to their case records and files consistent with applicable statutes regarding the procedures and conditions for reviewing these materials. Exceptions should be based on possible harm to the inmate or others.

Part One. Administration and Management

Release of Information

3-ALDF-1E-05
(Ref. 2-5106)

The facility uses a release of information consent form that complies with applicable federal and state regulations. Unless the release of information is required by statute, the inmate signs the consent form prior to the release of information, and a copy of the form is maintained in the inmate's case record.

Comment:
The confidentiality of information regarding inmates is protected by law. The consent form may include the following items: name of person and agency or organization requesting information; name of facility releasing information; specific information to be disclosed and purpose of disclosure; signature of inmate and date of signature; and signature of employee witnessing the inmate's signature. Where statutes direct, consent forms should not be required for release of information to judicial, law enforcement, correctional, and social service authorities involved with the individual case.

3-ALDF-1E-06
(Ref. 2-5103)

Written policy and procedure provide that a current and accurate classification or case record is maintained for each inmate committed to or housed in the facility. Procedures are established to safeguard legally privileged or confidential information. The records contain, at a minimum:

- **classification and reclassification decisions**
- **reports of disciplinary actions, grievances, incidents, and crimes committed while in custody**
- **medical and mental health information relevant to classification**
- **information on work or study release, when applicable**

Comment:
Case records should be seen as a resource in case decisionmaking, custody assignment, and program planning. Case records frequently contain privileged information and must be separate from custody records, according to statute. Written policy and procedure should clearly indicate the record in which information should be recorded and where documents should be filed. The inmate's grievance file may be maintained separately from the inmate's case record file, but in a centralized location where it is readily available to administrative staff with a need to know.

Section F
Information Systems and Research

Principle: A written body of policy and procedure establishes the facility's procedures for information storage and retrieval, master indexes, daily reports, evaluation, and research.

Information System

3-ALDF-1F-01
(Ref. 2-5090)
The facility contributes to, has access to, and uses an organized system of information storage, retrieval, and review. The information system is part of an overall research and decision-making capacity relating to both inmate and operational needs.

Comment:
Correctional information systems facilitate decision making, research, and timely responses to offender needs and outside inquiries. In large correctional systems, information systems often are the responsibility of the parent agency. If the parent agency does not provide this function, the facility should train and assign specific personnel to this function.

3-ALDF-1F-02
(Ref. 2-5105)
All staff who have direct access to information in the information system are trained in and responsive to the system's security requirements.

Comment:
Written policy should specify which persons have direct access to the information system.

Sharing of Information

3-ALDF-1F-03
(Ref. 2-5092)
The facility or parent agency collaborates with criminal justice and service agencies in information gathering, exchange, and standardization.

Comment:
Systemwide collaboration is critical to effective management and timely decisionmaking and helps prevent or reduce duplication of effort and costs. Facilities should share information among themselves while respecting the confidentiality and privacy of offender records.

Master Index and Daily Reports

3-ALDF-1F-04
(Ref. 2-5094)
Written policy and procedure provide for an inmate population accounting system that includes records on the admission, processing, and release of inmates.

Comment:
None.

Part One. Administration and Management

3-ALDF-1F-05
(Ref. 2-5104)

The facility maintains a system that identifies all inmates in custody and their actual physical locations.

Comment:
None.

3-ALDF-1F-06
(Ref. 2-5175)

The facility administration maintains a written record of the following:

- personnel on duty
- inmate population count
- admissions and releases of inmates
- shift activities
- entry and exit of physicians, attorneys, and other visitors
- unusual occurrences

Comment:
None.

3-ALDF-1F-07
(Ref. 2-5099)

Intake booking information is recorded for every person admitted to the facility and includes at least the following data, unless prohibited by law:

- picture
- booking number
- name and aliases of person
- current address (or last known address)
- date, duration of confinement, and a copy of the court order or other legal basis for commitment
- name, title and signature of delivering officer
- specific charge(s)
- sex
- age
- date of birth
- place of birth
- race
- present or last place of employment
- health status, including any current medical or mental health needs
- emergency contact (name, relation, address and phone number)
- driver's license and social security numbers
- notation of cash and all property
- additional information concerning special custody requirements, service needs, or other identifying information such as birthmark or tattoos

Comment:
None.

Section F. Information Systems and Research

3-ALDF-1F-08
(Ref. 2-5101)
The facility maintains custody records on all inmates committed or assigned to the facility, which include but are not limited to the following:

- **intake/booking information**
- **court-generated background information**
- **cash and property receipts**
- **reports of disciplinary actions, incidents, or crime(s) committed while in custody**
- **records of program participation, including work release or trusty programs and "good time" accumulated**

Comment:
None.

Conduct of Research

3-ALDF-1F-09
(Ref. 2-5096)
Written policy and procedure govern the conduct of research in the facility, including compliance with professional and scientific ethics and with state and federal guidelines for the use and dissemination of research findings.

Comment:
Researchers working in the facility should be informed about all policies relating to their research, especially those regarding confidentiality of information. Research results should be available to the warden/superintendent for review and comment before dissemination or publication.

3-ALDF-1F-10
(Ref. 2-5097)
The facility administrator reviews and approves all facility research projects prior to implementation to ensure they conform with the policies of the parent agency.

Comment:
The research design and the requirements that will be made of staff should be fully understood and agreed on before any research project proceeds.

Inmate Participation

3-ALDF-1F-11
(Ref. 2-5098)
Written policy and procedure govern voluntary inmate participation in nonmedical, nonpharmaceutical, and noncosmetic research programs.

Comment:
None.

Section G
Citizen Involvement and Volunteers

Principle: A written body of policy and procedure establishes the responsibility, screening, training, and operating procedures for a citizen involvement and volunteer program.

Program Coordination

3-ALDF-1G-01
(Ref. 2-5385)
The facility has a qualified staff person who coordinates the volunteer services program.

Comment:
This position may be full-time or part-time and may be filled by volunteer or contract personnel. If the person is not trained in volunteer services, he/she should receive appropriate training.

3-ALDF-1G-02
(Ref. 2-5377)
Written policy and procedure specify the lines of authority, responsibility, and accountability for the facility's citizen involvement and volunteer services program.

Comment:
Written policy should provide direction for the program, listing the goals and objectives, types of services offered, population served, etc. Clear lines of accountability and authority should be established and communicated to staff and volunteers. Any volunteer activity that is shown to threaten the facility's order and security or the safety of a volunteer should be limited or discontinued until the problem is resolved.

Screening and Selection

3-ALDF-1G-03
(Ref. 2-5387)
The screening and selection of volunteers allows for recruitment from all cultural and socioeconomic parts of the community.

Comment:
Efforts should be made to recruit volunteers from all segments of society. Volunteers should be selected on the basis of a uniform screening process that is consistent with security concerns.

Registration

3-ALDF-1G-04
(Ref. 2-5389)
There is an official registration and identification system for volunteers.

Comment:
All volunteers should be registered with the facility or parent agency for insurance purposes, and each volunteer should be issued an identification card. The facility should maintain an identification record for each volunteer that includes a photograph, address, current telephone number, and other relevant information.

Offer of Professional Services

3-ALDF-1G-05 Written policy specifies that volunteers may perform professional services only
(Ref. 2-5391) when they are certified, licensed, or qualified to do so.

Comment:
Volunteers who wish to offer professional services should be asked to cite their credentials and/or certificate status in their initial application. Tutoring or sponsorship of a craft or hobby program is not considered a professional service.

Orientation and Training

3-ALDF-1G-06 Written policy, procedure, and practice provide that each volunteer completes an
(Ref. 2-5388) appropriate, documented orientation and/or training program prior to assignment.

Comment:
None.

3-ALDF-1G-07 Volunteers agree in writing to abide by all facility policies, particularly those
(Ref. 2-5390) relating to the security and confidentiality of information.

Comment:
Confidentiality of records and of other privileged information is critical to facility security. The facility should develop written policies and procedures specifying that volunteers respect all facility policies.

Schedule of Services

3-ALDF-1G-08 A current schedule of volunteer services is available to all inmates and is posted
(Ref. New) in appropriate areas of the facility.

Comment:
None.

Participation in Policy Making

3-ALDF-1G-09 There is provision for volunteers to contribute suggestions regarding the estab-
(Ref. New) lishment of policy and procedure for the volunteer services program.

Comment:
None.

Part Two
Physical Plant

Unless otherwise noted, each standard applies to existing facilities, renovations, additions, and/or new plant construction. "New construction" is for final plans approved after January 1, 1992.

Section A
Building and Safety Codes

Principle: Compliance with professional building and fire safety codes helps to ensure the safety of all persons within the facility.

Building Codes

3-ALDF-2A-01
(Ref. 2-5134)

The facility conforms to applicable federal, state, and/or local building codes. (Renovation, addition, new construction only)

Comment:
Conformance with codes is indicated by licensing or, in cases where a license is not issued, by letters or certificates of compliance. If the agency is not subject to local building codes, appropriate state or national codes must be applied.

Fire Codes

3-ALDF-2A-02
(Ref. 2-5136, 2-5149)
Mandatory

The facility conforms to applicable federal, state, and/or local fire safety codes. Compliance is documented by the authority having jurisdiction. A fire alarm and automatic detection system are required, as approved by the authority having jurisdiction, or there is a plan for addressing these or other deficiencies within a reasonable time period. The authority approves any variances, exceptions, or equivalencies that do not constitute a serious life safety threat to the occupants of the facility.

Comment:
The applicable fire safety code(s) must be comprehensive, ensure basic protection of life, and include the use of fire detection and alarm systems in all habitable areas of the facility. The applicable code(s) should be applied to all areas of the facility. Reports of periodic inspections and any actions taken in respect to those inspections must be available.

Section B
Size, Organization, and Location

Principle: The question of facility size is most accurately approached from the perspective of the individual units that make up the facility. This approach encourages flexibility, creativity, and innovation in meeting concerns for safety and quality of life.

Staff/Inmate Interaction

3-ALDF-2B-01
(Ref. 2-5134-1)

Physical plant design facilitates continuous personal contact and interaction between staff and inmates in the housing unit.
(Renovation, addition, new construction only)

Comment:
Separation of supervising staff from inmates reduces interpersonal relationships and staff awareness of conditions on the housing unit. Staff effectiveness is limited if the only staff available are isolated in control centers as observers or technicians in charge of electronic management systems.

3-ALDF-2B-02
(Ref. 2-5141)

The facility is designed and constructed so that inmates can be separated according to existing laws and regulations or according to the facility's classification plan.
(Addition, new plant)

Comment:
None.

Unit Size

3-ALDF-2B-03
(Ref. 2-5135-1)

Written policy and procedure require that all living areas are constructed to facilitate continuous staff observation, excluding electronic surveillance, of cell or detention room fronts and areas such as dayrooms and recreation spaces.
(Renovation, addition, new plant)

Comment:
Continuous observation of inmate living areas is a fundamental requirement for maintaining safe, secure custody and control. The physical plant should facilitate the performance of this operational function.

Rated Capacity

3-ALDF-2B-04
(Ref. New)

The number of inmates does not exceed the facility's rated bed capacity.

Comment:
Rated bed capacity is considered to be the original design capacity, plus or minus capacity changes resulting from building additions, reductions, or revisions.

Location

3-ALDF-2B-05
(Ref. 2-5140)
The facility is geographically accessible to criminal justice agencies, community agencies, and inmates' lawyers, families, and friends.
(New plant)

Comment:
None.

Section C
Inmate Housing

Principle: Inmate housing areas are the foundation of institutional living and must promote the safety and well-being of both inmates and staff.

Inmate Sleeping Areas

Occupancy and Space Requirements

3-ALDF-2C-01
(Ref. 2-5110,
2-5111)

Single cells are required for maximum security inmates. All cells or sleeping areas in which inmates are confined contain 35 square feet of unencumbered space. When confinement exceeds 10 hours per day, there is at least 80 square feet of total floor space per occupant.

"Unencumbered space" is usable space that is not encumbered by furnishings or fixtures. At least one dimension of the unencumbered space is no less than seven feet. In determining unencumbered space, all fixtures must be in operational position and must provide the following minimum areas per person: bed, plumbing fixtures, desk, and locker.

Comment:
The standard encourages design flexibility and creativity by relating cell size to the amount of unencumbered, or free, space provided by the design. Unencumbered space is determined by multiplying the length and width of the cell/room and subtracting from that figure the total number of square feet encumbered by bed(s), plumbing fixtures, desk(s), locker(s), and other fixed equipment. Measurements should be made with equipment and furnishing in their normal use position (i.e., to discourage Murphy beds).

Furnishings

3-ALDF-2C-02
(Ref. 2-5112)

Each inmate confined to a cell/room for 10 or more hours daily is provided a sleeping area with the following: a sleeping surface and mattress at least 12 inches off of the floor; a writing surface and proximate area to sit; storage for personal items; and a place to suspend clothes.

Comment:
None.

Existing, Renovation, Addition, New Plant

3-ALDF-2C-03
(Ref. 2-5114)

When used for minimum or medium security inmates, multiple occupancy rooms house no less than two and no more than 50 inmates each who are screened prior to admission for suitability to group living. The rooms provide 35 square feet of unencumbered space per occupant. Sleeping partitions are required if more than four people are in one sleeping area. "Unencumbered space" is usable space that is not encumbered by furnishings or fixtures. At least one dimension of the unencumbered space is no less than seven feet.

Comment:
None.

3-ALDF-2C-04
(Ref. New)

At a minimum, the facility is designed to provide single-occupancy cells for one-third of the population.

Comment:
Good security, control, and programmatic practices require that facility administrators have adequate housing options available. In specialized units, the single-cell ratio may often demand additional single-celling.

Space Requirements

Dayrooms

3-ALDF-2C-05
(Ref. 2-5124, 2-5144)

Dayrooms with space for varied inmate activities are situated immediately adjacent to the inmate sleeping areas.

Dayrooms provide a minimum of 35 square feet of space per inmate (exclusive of lavatories, showers, and toilets) for the maximum number of inmates who use the dayroom at one time, and no dayroom encompasses less than 100 square feet of space (exclusive of lavatories, showers, and toilets).

Comment:
While the standard establishes a minimum square footage for any dayroom, total square footage is calculated for the maximum number of users at one time rather than the total number of inmates served.

3-ALDF-2C-06
(Ref. 2-5128)

There is at least one multipurpose room available for inmate activities such as religious services, education programs, or visiting.
(Existing, renovation, addition, new plant)

Comment:
None.

3-ALDF-2C-07
(Ref. New)

Dayrooms provide sufficient seating and writing surfaces for every inmate using the dayroom at one time. Dayroom furnishings are consistent with the custody level of the inmates assigned.

Comment:
The standard provides managers and designers with flexibility in designing and furnishing dayrooms and takes into consideration the range of activities that may occur (e.g., television viewing, reading, recreation, conversation, games, and sometimes meals and work). In lower security settings, the use of "normalized" furnishings should be considered.

Part Two. Physical Plant

Toilets

3-ALDF-2C-08
(Ref. 2-5112)

Inmates have access to toilets and hand-washing facilities 24 hours per day and are able to use toilet facilities without staff assistance when they are confined in their cells/sleeping areas.

Toilets are provided at a minimum ratio of one for every 12 inmates in male facilities and one for every eight inmates in female facilities. Urinals may be substituted for up to one-half of the toilets in male facilities. All housing units with three or more inmates have a minimum of two toilets.

Comment:
The standard ensures the availability of toilets and requires a measure of privacy and control for users. At the same time, the standard provides flexibility for designers and managers, who have increased options for "dry" cells if toilet facilities are accessible by other means (e.g., push-button locks on cells for use during the night). Creative design approaches that increase privacy and decrease management problems associated with congregate facilities (e.g., creation of a series of "single occupancy" toilet areas) are encouraged.

Wash Basins

3-ALDF-2C-09
(Ref. New)

Inmates have access to operable wash basins with hot and cold running water in the housing units at a minimum ratio of one basin for every 12 occupants.

Comment:
Provision must be made for inmate access in cells or sleeping areas, dayrooms, and other parts of the facility.

Showers

3-ALDF-2C-10
(Ref. 2-5112)

Inmates have access to operable showers with temperature-controlled hot and cold running water at a minimum ratio of one shower for every eight inmates. Water for showers is thermostatically controlled to temperatures ranging from 100 degrees to 120 degrees Fahrenheit to ensure the safety of inmates and to promote hygienic practice.

Comment:
Offenders can use scalding showers as a weapon against, or punishment for, other inmates. Also, accidental injury could occur when cold water is drawn in other areas, thereby unexpectedly elevating the hot water in showers to scalding temperatures. Water temperatures below 100 degrees Fahrenheit are uncomfortable and may deter an individual from pursuing good hygienic practices. The temperature controls should not preclude the use of water at higher temperatures, if needed, in other areas of the facility, such as kitchens.

Section C. Inmate Housing

Special Management Housing

3-ALDF-2C-11
(Ref. 2-5115, 2-5116)
Segregation housing units provide living conditions that approximate those of the general inmate population; all exceptions are clearly documented. Segregation cells/rooms permit the inmates assigned to them to converse with and be observed by staff members.

Comment:
None.

3-ALDF-2C-12
(Ref. 2-5115)
All cells/rooms in segregation provide a minimum of 80 square feet, of which 35 square feet is unencumbered space.

Comment:
None.

Housing for the Handicapped

3-ALDF-2C-13
(Ref. 2-5142)
Handicapped inmates are housed in a manner that provides for their safety and security. Rooms, cells, or housing units used by the handicapped are designed for their use and provide for integration with the general population. Appropriate facility programs and activities are accessible to handicapped inmates confined in the facility.

Comment:
If the facility accepts handicapped individuals, it must provide for their housing and use of facility resources.

3-ALDF-2C-14
(Ref. 2-5383)
Inmates participating in work or educational release programs are separated from inmates in the general population.

Comment:
None.

Section D
Environmental Conditions

Principle: Environmental conditions significantly influence the overall effectiveness of facility operations. Standards for lighting, air quality, temperature, and noise levels are designed to preserve the health and well-being of inmates and staff members and to promote facility order and security.

Light Levels

General

3-ALDF-2D-01
(Ref. New)

Lighting throughout the facility is determined by the tasks to be performed, interior surface finishes and colors, type and spacing of light sources, outside lighting, and shadows and glare.

Comment:
None.

Inmate Rooms/Cells

3-ALDF-2D-02
(Ref. 2-5112)

Lighting in inmate rooms/cells is at least 20 footcandles at desk level and in personal grooming areas, as documented by an independent, qualified source.

Comment:
None.

Natural Light

Inmate Rooms/Cells

3-ALDF-2D-03
(Ref. New)

All inmate rooms/cells provide access to natural light.
(Existing, renovation, addition only)

Comment:
None.

3-ALDF-2D-04
(Ref. 2-5112, 2-5115)

Inmates in the general population who are confined in their rooms/cells for 10 or more hours daily have access to natural light by means of an opening or window of at least three square feet with a view to the outside.

Inmates in the general population who are confined in their rooms/cells for less than 10 hours daily have access to natural light through an opening or window as described above or through an opening or window of at least three square feet between their room/cell and an adjacent space.
(New construction only)

Comment:
None.

Section D. Environmental Conditions

Dayrooms

3-ALDF-2D-05
(Ref. New)
Each dayroom provides a minimum of 12 square feet of transparent glazing with a view to the outside, plus two additional square feet of glazing per inmate whose room/cell does not contain an opening or window with a view to the outside.

Comment:
Many inmates spend most daylight hours outside of their cells, often in the dayroom, and the standard gives designers increased options for providing natural light.

3-ALDF-2D-06
(Ref. 2-5112)
Noise levels in inmate housing units do not exceed 70 dBA (A Scale) in daytime and 45 dBA (A Scale) at night.

Comment:
None.

Indoor Air Quality

3-ALDF-2D-07
(Ref. New)
Written policy, procedure, and practice provide that a ventilation system is provided that supplies at least 15 cubic feet per minute of circulated air per occupant with a minimum of five cubic feet per minute of outside air. Toilet rooms and cells with toilets shall have no less than four airchanges per hour. Air quantities shall be documented by a qualified independent source.

Comment:
The required air quantities shall be provided when the building or portion of the building is occupied.

3-ALDF-2D-08
(Ref. New)
Written policy, procedure, and practice govern the smoking practices of all persons in the facility and designate appropriate smoking and nonsmoking areas.

Comment:
An increasing body of medical research indicates a need for control of smoking practices.

Heating and Cooling

3-ALDF-2D-09
(Ref. 2-5112)
Temperatures in indoor living and work areas are appropriate to the summer and winter comfort zones.

Comment:
Temperature and humidity should be capable of being mechanically raised or lowered to acceptable comfort levels.

Section E
Program and Service Areas

Principle: Adequate space must be provided for the various program and service functions conducted within the facility. Spatial requirements are best determined by careful assessment of how, when, and by how many inmates such spaces are used.

Exercise and Recreation

3-ALDF-2E-01
(Ref. 2-5125)

Outdoor and covered/enclosed exercise areas for general population inmates are provided in sufficient number to ensure that each inmate is offered at least one hour of access daily. Use of outdoor areas is preferred, but covered/enclosed areas must be available for use in inclement weather. Covered/enclosed exercise areas can be designed for multiple uses as long as the design and furnishings do not interfere with scheduled exercise activities.

The minimum space requirements for exercise areas are as follows:

- outdoor exercise areas—15 square feet per inmate for the maximum number of inmates expected to use the space at one time, but not less than 1,500 square feet of unencumbered space
- covered/enclosed exercise areas in facilities of 100 or more inmates—15 square feet per inmate for the maximum number of inmates expected to use the space at one time, with a minimum ceiling height of 18 feet, but not less than 1,000 square feet of unencumbered space
- covered/enclosed exercise areas in facilities of less than 100 inmates—15 square feet per inmate for the maximum number of inmates expected to use the space at one time, with a minimum ceiling height of 18 feet, but not less than 500 square feet of unencumbered space

Comment:
Exercise/recreation spaces are not the same as dayrooms, although dayrooms can provide additional opportunities for some exercise and recreation activities. The standard establishes performance requirements for exercise spaces, offering design and operational flexibility. It allows facilities in some climates to cover and/or enclose a yard, while others will have to provide indoor space; these spaces do not have to be "indoor" but must be fully functional when the outdoor areas are not feasible for use.

3-ALDF-2E-02
(Ref. 2-5144)

The minimum space requirements for outdoor and covered/enclosed exercise areas for segregation units are 15 square feet per inmate expected to use the space at one time, with a minimum ceiling height of 18 feet in covered/enclosed areas, but not less than 500 square feet of unencumbered space.

Comment:
None.

Visiting

3-ALDF-2E-03
(Ref. New)
Sufficient space is provided for a visiting room and contact visiting when appropriate. There is adequately designed space to permit appropriate screening and searching of both inmates and visitors. Space is provided for the storage of visitors' coats, handbags, and other personal items not allowed into the visiting area.

Comment:
None.

Classrooms

3-ALDF-2E-04
(Ref. New)
In facilities offering academic and vocational training programs, classrooms are designed in consultation with school authorities.
(Renovation, addition, new construction only)

Comment:
Space requirements that afford safety and mobility are necessary in both the educational and vocational areas.

Dining

3-ALDF-2E-05
(Ref. New)
Dining space is sufficient to serve all inmates in four or fewer shifts per meal while giving each inmate the opportunity to have at least 20 minutes of dining time for each meal.

Comment:
None.

Food Service

Food Preparation Areas

3-ALDF-2E-06
(Ref. 2-5126)
The food preparation area includes a space for food preparation based on population size, type of food preparation, and methods of meal service.

Comment:
None.

Food Storage

3-ALDF-2E-07
(Ref. 2-5241)
There are sanitary, temperature-controlled facilities for the storage of all foods.

Comment:
None.

Part Two. Physical Plant

Sanitation and Hygiene

3-ALDF-2E-08
(Ref. 2-5235)
Toilet and wash basin facilities are available to food service personnel and inmates in the vicinity of the food preparation area.

Comment:
None.

Housekeeping

3-ALDF-2E-09
(Ref. 2-5130)
Adequate space is provided for janitorial closets accessible to the living and activity areas. The closets are equipped with a sink and cleaning implements.

Comment:
None.

Clothing and Supplies

3-ALDF-2E-10
(Ref. New)
Space is provided in the facility to store and issue clothing, bedding, cleaning supplies, and other items required for daily operations.

Comment:
None.

Personal Property

3-ALDF-2E-11
(Ref. 2-5131)
Space is provided for storing the personal property of inmates safely and securely.

Comment:
None.

Mechanical Equipment

3-ALDF-2E-12
(Ref. 2-5148)
Separate and adequate space is provided for mechanical and electrical equipment.

Comment:
None.

Commissary/Canteen

3-ALDF-2E-13
(Ref. New)
Space is provided for an inmate commissary or canteen, or provisions are made for a commissary service.

Comment:
None.

Section F
Administrative and Staff Areas

Principle: All levels of staff must be provided with adequate space to carry out their responsibilities safely and effectively.

Administrative Areas

3-ALDF-2F-01 **Adequate space is provided for administrative, security, professional, and clerical staff; this space includes conference rooms, storage room for records, public lobby, and toilet facilities.**
(Ref. 2-5127)

Comment:
None.

Staff Areas

3-ALDF-2F-02 **Staff needs are met through providing adequate spaces in locations that are convenient for use. Staff are provided with the following:**
(Ref. 2-5127)

- **an area to change clothes and to shower**
- **an area, room, and/or employee lounge that offers privacy from inmates and provides space for meals**
- **access to exercise/physical training facilities and equipment**
- **space for training**
- **space for shift change briefings**
- **toilets and wash basins that are not used by inmates**

Comment:
Facilities are appropriate for male and female staff.

Accessibility to the Handicapped

3-ALDF-2F-03 **All parts of the facility that are accessible to the public are accessible to and usable by handicapped staff and visitors.**
(Ref. 2-5143)

Comment:
None.

Section G
Security

Principle: The physical plant supports the orderly and secure functioning of the facility.

Control Center

3-ALDF-2G-01
(Ref. 2-5164)

Space is provided for a 24-hour control center for monitoring and coordinating the facility's security, life safety, and communications systems. The control center provides access to a wash basin and toilet.

Comment:
The control center should contain sufficient space for monitoring and coordination of all internal and external security systems, communications systems, safety alarms and detection systems, and other mechanical and electrical systems.

Perimeter Security

3-ALDF-2G-02
(Ref. New)

The facility's perimeter is controlled by appropriate means to provide that inmates remain within the perimeter and to prevent access by the general public without proper authorization.

Comment:
The means chosen to ensure perimeter security should reflect the facility's needs based on size and the degree of security required. Some methods are perimeter surveillance devices (e.g., electronic, pressure, or sound detection systems), mobile patrols, or a combination of these techniques. All areas adjacent to the perimeter should be visible under all conditions.

Entrances and Exits

3-ALDF-2G-03
(Ref. New)

Pedestrians and vehicles enter and leave at designated points in the perimeter. Safety vestibules and sally ports constitute the only breaches in the perimeter.

Comment:
None.

Security Equipment Storage

3-ALDF-2G-04
(Ref. 2-5184)

Firearms, chemical agents, and related security items are stored in a secure but readily accessible depository outside of inmate housing and activity areas.

Comment:
None.

3-ALDF-2G-05
(Ref. 2-5120)
Mandatory

The facility has exits that are properly positioned, clear, and distinctly and permanently marked to ensure the timely evacuation of inmates and staff in the event of fire or other emergency. All housing areas and places of assembly for 50 or more persons have two exits.
(Existing, renovation, addition, new plant)

Comment:
Emergency exits should be provided to ensure the safety of inmates, staff, and visitors. The exits should be positioned in such a manner that if one exit is blocked by fire and/or smoke, the other exit is available. All exits should be continuously visible at all times, kept clear and free of obstructions, and maintained in a usable condition. They should lead directly to a hazard-free area where adequate supervision can be provided. Battery-operated electric lights, portable lamps, or lanterns should not be used for primary illumination of exits. Electric battery-operated lighting may be used as an emergency source where normal lighting has failed, as defined in the National Fire Protection Association's National Electrical Code. These requirements also apply to exits in buildings designed for public or common use.

Part Three
Institutional Operations

Section A
Security and Control

Principle: The facility uses a combination of supervision, inspection, accountability, and clearly-defined policies and procedures on use of weapons and force to promote safe and orderly operations.

Security Manual

3-ALDF-3A-01
(Ref. 2-5163)

There is a manual containing all procedures for facility security and control, with detailed instructions for implementing these procedures. The manual is available to all staff, reviewed at least annually, and updated if necessary.

Comment:
The manual should contain information on physical plant inspection; inmate counts; weapons and chemical agent control; contraband; key control; tool and equipment control; and emergency procedures.

Control Center

3-ALDF-3A-02
Ref. 2-5165)

The facility has a communication system between the control center and inmate living areas.

Comment:
A mechanical or audio communication system should be used to supplement direct staff supervision activities (e.g., to advise staff of emergency needs), not as a substitute for staff supervision.

Correctional Officer Assignments

3-ALDF-3A-03
(Ref. 2-5173)

Correctional officer posts are located in or immediately adjacent to inmate living areas to permit officers to hear and respond promptly to emergency situations. The assisting officer may be physically available or within sight or sound of the officer entering the unit.

Comment:
The presence of correctional officers within hearing distance of inmate living quarters can help prevent inmate misbehavior and avoid disturbances. The assisting officer should be able to provide assistance personally or to summon emergency assistance from others.

Part Three. Institutional Operations

3-ALDF-3A-04 The facility has the staff needed to provide full coverage of designated security
(Ref. 2-5172) posts, full surveillance of inmates, and to perform all ancillary functions.

Comment:
None.

3-ALDF-3A-05 There are written orders for every correctional officer post. These orders are
(Ref. 2-5192) reviewed annually and updated if necessary.

Comment:
Written orders should specify the duties of each post and the procedures to be followed to carry out the assignment. Copies of the post orders should be available for all employees.

3-ALDF-3A-06 Written policy, procedure, and practice provide that personnel read the ap-
(Ref. 2-5193) propriate post order each time they assume a new post and sign and date the post order.

Comment:
None.

3-ALDF-3A-07 Written policy, procedure, and practice facilitate personal contact and interac-
(Ref. 2-5171-1) tion between staff and inmates.

Comment:
Staff effectiveness is limited if the only staff available are placed in isolated control centers during periods of inmate activity in the housing units.

3-ALDF-3A-08 Written policy, procedure, and practice require that when both males and females
(Ref. 2-5171-2) are housed in the facility, at least one male and one female staff member are on duty at all times.

Comment:
None.

3-ALDF-3A-09 Written policy, procedure, and practice provide that no inmate or group of
(Ref. 2-5200) inmates is given control or authority over other inmates.

Comment:
None.

Section A. Security and Control

Permanent Log

3-ALDF-3A-10
(Ref. 2-5201)
Written policy, procedure, and practice require that correctional staff maintain a permanent log and prepare shift reports that record routine information, emergency situations, and unusual incidents.

Comment:
Adequate supervision of inmates requires a formal, written reporting system. Each correctional officer in each housing unit on each shift should maintain detailed records of pertinent information regarding individual inmates and groups of inmates.

Patrols and Inspections

3-ALDF-3A-11
(Ref. 2-5176)
Written policy, procedure, and practice provide that supervisory staff conduct a daily patrol, including holidays and weekends, of all areas occupied by inmates and submit a daily written report to their supervisor. Unoccupied areas are to be inspected weekly.

Comment:
Matters requiring further attention (e.g., staff and inmate concerns; faulty, unsafe, or dirty conditions) should be reported in writing for review and further action.

3-ALDF-3A-12
(Ref. 2-5177)
Written policy, procedure, and practice require that the facility administrator or designee, assistant facility administrator, and designated department heads visit the facility's living and activity areas at least weekly to encourage informal contact with staff and inmates and to informally observe living and working conditions.

Comment:
Arrangements should be made for inmates to have informal access to key staff. This can be achieved through staff visits to the housing units, work areas, educational and recreational areas, and other areas in the facility where inmates can be contacted during the day or evening. Policy should specify which department heads are expected to make at least weekly visits and should encourage other department heads and supervisory staff to visit these areas as often as practical.

3-ALDF-3A-13
(Ref. 2-5177)
Written policy, procedure, and practice require that the chief security officer or qualified designee conduct at least weekly inspections of all security devices needing repair or maintenance and report the results of the inspections in writing.

Comment:
There should be a scheduled maintenance procedure to ensure that all bars, locks, windows, doors, and other security devices are fully operational. Emergency keys should be checked at least quarterly to ensure they are in working order. The results of all inspections should be submitted in writing to the facility administrator and/or the officer in charge of security.

Part Three. Institutional Operations

Inmate Counts

3-ALDF-3A-14
(Ref. 2-5178)

The facility has a system for physically counting inmates. The system includes strict accountability for inmates assigned to work and educational release, furloughs, and other approved temporary absences.

Comment:
There should be at least one inmate count per shift. Counts should be scheduled so that they do not conflict with activity programs and normal operating procedures. The officer responsible for maintaining the master count record should have up-to-the-minute information regarding all inmate housing modules, work assignment changes, hospital admissions, etc. Adequate checks should be instituted to allow for human error. All inmates in legal custody should be accounted for in the master count; all temporary absences from the facility should be explained in writing.

Inmate Movement

3-ALDF-3A-15
(Ref. 2-5170)

Written policy, procedure, and practice provide that staff regulate inmate movement.

Comment:
All inmate movement from one location to another should be controlled and supervised by staff, including individual and group inmate movement to and from work and program assignments. A master pass list for each day can assist in accounting for movement without restricting or discouraging participation in program activities.

3-ALDF-3A-16
(Ref. 2-5203)

Written policy and procedure govern the transportation of inmates outside the facility and from one jurisdiction to another.

Comment:
Guidelines for transporting inmates should emphasize safety and should be made available to all personnel involved in transporting inmates. The facility should have policies governing the use of restraints.

Use of Restraints

3-ALDF-3A-17
(Ref. 2-5199)

Written policy, procedure, and practice provide that instruments of restraint, such as handcuffs, irons, and straightjackets, are never applied as punishment and are applied only with the approval of the facility administrator or designee.

Comment:
Instruments of restraint should be used only as a precaution against escape during transfer; for medical reasons; by direction of the medical officer; or to prevent self-injury, injury to others, or property damage. Restraints should not be applied for more time than is absolutely necessary.

Section A. Security and Control

Control of Contraband

3-ALDF-3A-18
(Ref. 2-5179)
Written policy, procedure, and practice provide for searches of facilities and inmates to control contraband and provide for its disposition. These policies are made available to staff and inmates; policies and procedures are reviewed at least annually and updated if necessary.

Comment:
None.

3-ALDF-3A-19
(Ref. 2-5180)
Written policy, procedure, and practice provide that manual or instrument inspection of body cavities is conducted only when there is reason to do so and when authorized by the facility administrator or designee. The inspection is conducted in private by health care personnel or correctional personnel trained by health care personnel.

Comment:
None.

3-ALDF-3A-20
(Ref. 2-5180)
Written policy, procedure, and practice provide that visual inspection of inmate body cavities is conducted based on a reasonable belief that the inmate is carrying contraband or other prohibited material. The inspection is conducted by trained staff in private.

Comment:
Strip searches may be conducted following such activities as contact visiting, return to the facility from furlough, and other activities based on the security level of the inmate.

Part Three. Institutional Operations

Controlled Access and Use of Keys

3-ALDF-3A-21
(Ref. 2-5190) **Written policy and procedure govern the control and use of keys.**

Comment:
The key control system should provide a current accounting of the location and possessor of each key. All keys should be issued from the central control area, and a log should be used to record the number of each key issued, the location of the lock, the number of keys to that lock, and the names of all employees possessing a key.

Keys should be stored so that their presence or absence can be easily determined. Keys should be returned to the control center daily. All keys should be numbered, and the facility should maintain at least one duplicate key for each lock. Fire and emergency keys should be color-coded and marked for identification by touch. Inmates should not possess keys other than those to living quarters or work assignments, when appropriate, and to personal lockers.

Tools and Equipment

3-ALDF-3A-22
(Ref. 2-5191) **Written policy and procedure govern the control and use of tools and culinary and medical equipment.**

Comment:
Tools and utensils that can cause death or serious injury (e.g., hacksaws, welding equipment, butcher knives, barber shears) should be locked in control panels and issued in accordance with a prescribed system. Provision should be made for checking tools and utensils in and out to control their use at all times.

Vehicles

3-ALDF-3A-23
(Ref. 2-5204) **Written policy and procedure govern the use and security of facility vehicles.**

Comment:
None.

3-ALDF-3A-24
(Ref. 2-5205) **Written policy and procedure govern the use of personal vehicles for official purposes and include provisions for insurance coverage.**

Comment:
Written policy should specify the conditions for the official use of personal vehicles and the limits of facility liability.

Section A. Security and Control

Security Equipment

General Policies and Practice

3-ALDF-3A-25
(Ref. 2-5183)

Written policy and procedure govern the availability, control, and use of chemical agents, electrical disablers, and related security devices and specify the level of authority required for their access and use. Chemical agents and electrical disablers are used only with the authorization of the facility administrator or designee.

Comment:
Based on an analysis of the physical plant and the size and profile of the inmate population, designated staff should determine what firearms, chemical agents, electrical disablers, and other security devices (such as shields, batons, helmets, gloves, and body protectors) the facility needs. Written policies and procedures should specify the level of authority required for access to and use of security devices.

3-ALDF-3A-26
(Ref. 2-5186)

Written policy, procedure, and practice provide that the facility maintains a written record of routine and emergency distributions of security equipment.

Comment:
The written record should detail who receives security equipment and what equipment they receive.

3-ALDF-3A-27
(Ref. 2-5184)

Firearms, chemical agents, and related security equipment are inventoried at least monthly to determine their condition and expiration dates.

Comment:
Written policy should specify who has access to the depository where the security equipment is stored.

3-ALDF-3A-28
(Ref. 2-5187)

Written policy, procedure, and practice require that personnel discharging firearms, using chemical agents or any other weapon, or using force to control inmates submit written reports to the facility administrator or designee no later than the conclusion of the tour of duty.

Comment:
All instances involving the discharge of firearms and use of chemical agents should be documented to establish the identity of the personnel and inmates involved and to describe the nature of the incident.

3-ALDF-3A-29
(Ref. 2-5188)
Mandatory

Written policy, procedure, and practice provide that all persons injured in an incident receive immediate medical examination and treatment.

Comment:
Immediate medical examination and treatment should be required in all instances involving the use of a weapon or chemical agent.

Part Three. Institutional Operations

Use of Firearms

3-ALDF-3A-30
(Ref. 2-5196)

Written policy, procedure, and practice provide for the safe unloading and reloading of firearms.

Comment:
There should be a process for the unloading and reloading of firearms for both facility personnel and visiting law enforcement officers to ensure that these actions present the least possible danger.

3-ALDF-3A-31
(Ref. 2-5198)
Mandatory

Written policy, procedure, and practice restrict the use of physical force to instances of justifiable self-defence, protection of others, protection of property, and prevention of escapes, and then only as a last resort and in accordance with appropriate statutory authority. In no event is physical force justifiable as punishment. A written report is prepared following all uses of force and is submitted to administrative staff for review.

Comment:
Correctional personnel should be prepared to justify their use of physical force. The phrase "as a last resort" may be defined through appropriate statutory authority.

3-ALDF-3A-32
(Ref. 2-5185)
Mandatory

Written policy and procedure govern the use of firearms and include the following requirements:

1. Weapons are subjected to stringent safety regulations and inspections.
2. A secure weapons locker is located outside the security perimeter of the facility.
3. Except in emergency situations, firearms and weapons such as nightsticks are permitted only in designated areas to which inmates have no access.
4. Employees supervising inmates outside the facility perimeter follow procedures for the security of weapons.
5. Employees are instructed to use deadly force only after other actions have been tried and found ineffective, unless the employee believes that a person's life is immediately threatened.
6. Employees on duty only use firearms or other security equipment that have been approved through the facility and only when directed by or authorized by the facility administrator.

Comment:
None.

Section B
Safety and Emergency Procedures

Principle: The facility adheres to all applicable safety and fire codes and has in place the equipment and procedures necessary in the event of a major emergency.

Fire Safety

3-ALDF-3B-01
(Ref. 2-5151)
Mandatory

Written policy and procedure specify the facility's fire prevention regulations and practices to ensure the safety of staff, inmates, and visitors. These include, but are not limited to, the following:

- provision for an adequate fire protection service
- a system of fire inspection and testing of equipment at least quarterly
- an annual inspection by local or state fire officials or other qualified person(s)
- availability of fire hoses or extinguishers at appropriate locations throughout the facility

Comment:
The facility should plan and execute all reasonable procedures for the prevention and prompt control of fire.

3-ALDF-3B-02
(Ref. 2-5150)
Mandatory

Written policy, procedure, and practice provide for a comprehensive and thorough monthly inspection of the facility by a qualified fire and safety officer for compliance with safety and fire prevention standards. There is a weekly fire and safety inspection of the facility by a qualified departmental staff member. This policy and procedure is reviewed annually and updated as needed.

Comment:
The "qualified departmental staff member" who conducts the weekly inspections may be a facility staff member who has received training in and is familiar with the safety and sanitation requirements of the jurisdiction. At a minimum, it is expected that the safety/sanitation specialist will provide on-the-job training regarding applicable regulations and inspections, including the use of checklists and the methods of documentation.

3-ALDF-3B-03
(Ref. 2-5153)
Mandatory

Specifications for the selection and purchase of facility furnishings indicate the fire safety performance requirements of the materials selected.

Comment:
Furnishings, mattresses, cushions, or other items of foamed plastics or foamed rubber (e.g., polyurethane, polystyrene) can pose a severe hazard due to high smoke production, rapid burning once ignited, and high heat release. Such materials should be subjected to careful fire safety evaluation before purchase or use. All polyurethane should be removed from living areas unless its use is approved in writing by the fire authority having jurisdiction. The fire authority should consider the flammability and toxicity characteristics of the products being evaluated.

Facility furnishings include draperies, curtains, furniture, mattresses and bedding, upholstered or cushioned furniture, wastebaskets, decorations, and similar materials that can burn. "Furnishings" applies to all living quarters. The standard requires that specifications be known, if available, at the time of selection; there are no standards mandating knowledge of fire performance characteristics of furnishings in the facility prior to implementation of the policy relating to this standard.

3-ALDF-3B-04
(Ref. 2-5154)
Mandatory

Facilities are equipped with noncombustible receptacles for smoking materials and separate containers for other combustible refuse at accessible locations throughout living quarters in the facility. Special containers are provided for flammable liquids and for rags used with flammable liquids. All receptacles and containers are emptied and cleaned daily.

Comment:
None.

Flammable, Toxic, and Caustic Materials

3-ALDF-3B-05
(Ref. 2-5162)
Mandatory

Written policy, procedure, and practice govern the control and use of all flammable, toxic, and caustic materials.

Comment:
The following definitions apply to this standard: *Flammable materials*—Liquids with a flash point below 100 degrees Fahrenheit; *Toxic materials*—Substances that through chemical reaction or mixture can produce possible injury or harm to the body by entering through the skin, digestive tract, or respiratory tract (e.g., zinc chromate paint, ammonia, chlorine, antifreeze, herbicides, pesticides); *Caustic materials*—Substances that can destroy or eat away by chemical reaction (e.g., lye, caustic soda, sulfuric acid). If a substance possesses more than one of the above properties, the safety requirements for all applicable properties should be considered.

All flammable, toxic, and caustic materials should be stored in secure areas that are inaccessible to inmates, and a prescribed system should be used to account for their distribution. Inmates should never possess such items unless under the close supervision of qualified staff.

Substances that do not contain one or more of the above properties but that are labeled "Keep Out of the Reach of Children" or "May Be Harmful If Swallowed" are not prohibited; their use and control, however, should be addressed by agency policy.

Emergency Power and Communications

3-ALDF-3B-06
(Ref. 2-5157)

The facility has the equipment necessary to maintain essential lights, power, and communications in an emergency.

Comment:
The facility should have emergency power units, either battery- or motor-driven, to provide essential lighting and life-sustaining functions within the facility and to maintain outside communications in an emergency.

3-ALDF-3B-07
(Ref. New)

Written policy, procedure, and practice provide for a communications system within the facility and between the facility and community in the event of urgent, special, or unusual incidents or emergency situations.

Comment:
The facility should have available walkie-talkies and/or a radio base station, receivers, and transmitters or other independent mechanical means of communication in order to maintain constant contact with the outside community if conventional means of communication are disrupted. Facilities located in areas subject to severe storms, tornadoes, or hurricanes should maintain a ready means of voice communication with the community.

Part Three. Institutional Operations

3-ALDF-3B-08
(Ref. 2-5133)

There is a written plan for preventive maintenance of the physical plant; the plan includes provisions for emergency repairs or replacement in life-threatening situations.

Comment:
Regular care and inspection of equipment is essential for safe and efficient operations. The preventive maintenance plan should be implemented by qualified staff or maintenance professionals.

3-ALDF-3B-09
(Ref. 2-5158)

Power generators are tested at least every two weeks, and other emergency equipment and systems are tested at least quarterly for effectiveness and are repaired or replaced if necessary.

Comment:
Emergency equipment, such as standby lighting, batteries, power generators, firefighting apparatus, communications systems, and alarms, should be checked frequently to ensure their reliability.

Emergency Plans

Staff Training

3-ALDF-3B-10
(Ref. 2-5161)
Mandatory

All facility personnel are trained in the implementation of written emergency plans.

Comment:
Review of all emergency plans should be an essential element of personnel training and retraining programs. New employees should be familiar with all emergency plans prior to permanent work assignment.

Section B. Safety and Emergency Procedures

Evacuation Procedures

3-ALDF-3B-11
(Ref. 2-5159)
Mandatory

There is a written evacuation plan to be used in the event of fire or major emergency. The plan is certified by an independent, outside inspector trained in the application of national fire safety codes and is reviewed annually, updated if necessary, and reissued to the local fire jurisdiction. The plan includes the following:

- location of building/room floor plans
- use of exit signs and directional arrows for traffic flow
- location of publicly posted plan
- at least quarterly drills in all facility locations, including administrative areas
- staff drills when evacuation of extremely dangerous inmates may not be included

Comment:
The evacuation plan should specify evacuation routes, subsequent disposition and housing of inmates, and provision for medical care or hospital transportation for injured inmates and/or staff. Fire drills should include evacuation of all inmates except when there is clear and convincing evidence that facility security is jeopardized; upon such showing, actual evacuation during drills is not required, although staff supervising such inmates should be required to perform their roles/activity in quarterly drills.

3-ALDF-3B-12
(Rev. 2-5160)
Mandatory

Written policy, procedure, and practice specify the means for the immediate release of inmates from locked areas in case of emergency and provide for a backup system.

Comment:
The responsibilities of personnel in an emergency situation should be clearly defined. Staff should be aware of the location and identification of keys and be knowledgeable about all evacuation routes. Inmates should receive instructions concerning emergency procedures.

The authority having jurisdiction must certify that locking arrangements allow for prompt release and/or that sufficient staff are available to operate locking devices when necessary. A "backup system" means that there is a manual backup if power-operated locks fail. A control station or other locations removed from the inmate living areas should be equipped with reliable, manual means for releasing locks on swinging and sliding doors to permit prompt release. If the facility has only a manual locking system, a staff plan for manually releasing locks must be in place.

Work Stoppage

3-ALDF-3B-13
(Ref. 2-5197)

There is a written plan that provides for continuing operations in the event of a work stoppage or other job action. Copies of this plan are available to appropriate supervisory personnel.

Comment:
A contingency plan for maintaining essential services might involve agreements with other law enforcement agencies, such as local or state police.

Part Three. Institutional Operations

Threats to Security

3-ALDF-3B-14
(Ref. 2-5195)
Mandatory

There are written plans that specify the procedures to be followed in situations that threaten facility security. Such situations include but are not limited to: riots; hunger strikes; disturbances; and the taking of hostages. These plans are made available to all applicable personnel, are reviewed at least annually, and updated as needed.

Comment:
The plans should designate the personnel who are to implement the procedures; when and which authorities and media should be notified; how the problem should be contained; and the procedures to be followed after the incident is quelled. The plan presupposes regular inspection and maintenance of any specialized equipment necessary to implement the procedures. All personnel should be familiar with the plans. Hospital and medical personnel should be involved in the formulation of the plans, since they are responsible for the safety of their patients.

Escapes

3-ALDF-3B-15
(Ref. 2-5195)

There are written procedures regarding escapes; these procedures are reviewed at least annually and updated if necessary.

Comment:
Specific procedures that can be used quickly when an escape occurs should be made available to all personnel. Procedures should include the following: prompt reporting of the escape to the facility administrator; mobilization of employees; implementation of a predetermined search plan; notification of law enforcement agencies, community groups, and relevant media; preparation of escape circulars for distribution and mailing; and, after apprehension of the escapee, prompt notification of all who were previously alerted to the escape.

Section C
Rules and Discipline

Principle: The facility's rules of conduct and sanctions and procedures for violations are defined in writing and communicated to all inmates and staff. Disciplinary procedures are carried out promptly and with respect for due process.

Rules of Conduct

3-ALDF-3C-01
(Ref. 2-5303, 2-5306)

Written rules of inmate conduct specify acts prohibited within the facility and penalties that can be imposed for various degrees of violation; the written rules are reviewed annually and updated if necessary.

Comment:
The rules should prohibit only observed behavior that can be shown clearly to have a direct, adverse effect on an inmate or on facility order and security. The rules also should specify the range of penalties that can be imposed for violations. Penalties should be proportionate to the importance of the rule and severity of the violation.

3-ALDF-3C-02
(Ref. New)

There is a written set of disciplinary procedures governing inmate rule violations. These are reviewed annually and updated if necessary.

Comment:
None.

3-ALDF-3C-03
(Ref. 2-5305, 2-5306)

A rulebook that contains all chargeable offenses, ranges of penalties, and disciplinary procedures is given to each inmate and staff member and is translated into those languages spoken by significant numbers of inmates. Signed acknowledgement of receipt of the rulebook is maintained in the inmate's file. When a literacy or language problem prevents an inmate from understanding the rulebook, a staff member or translator assists the inmate in understanding the rules.

Comment:
Written procedures should specify how the rules and regulations are issued and presented to new inmates. Rules and regulations governing inmate conduct are of limited value unless the inmate understands them. "Posting" the rulebook is unnecessary provided there is evidence each inmate receives a copy of the rules.

3-ALDF-3C-04
(Ref. 2-5307)

All personnel who work with inmates receive sufficient training so that they are thoroughly familiar with the rules of inmate conduct, the rationale for the rules, and the sanctions available.

Comment:
All facility personnel who work with inmates in any way should receive continuous in-service training to prevent discrepancies among staff members in interpretation or implementation of rules of conduct.

Part Three. Institutional Operations

Resolution of Minor Infractions

3-ALDF-3C-05
(Ref. 2-5308)
There are written guidelines for resolving minor inmate infractions that include a written statement of the rule violated and a hearing and decision within seven days—excluding weekends and holidays—by a person not involved in the rule violation; the inmate may waive the hearing.

Comment:
Minor infractions do not include infractions that are resolved through an informal process.

Criminal Violations

3-ALDF-3C-06
(Ref. 2-5314)
Written policy, procedure, and practice provide that, where an inmate allegedly commits an act covered by criminal law, the case is referred to appropriate court or law enforcement officials for consideration for prosecution.

Comment:
Corrections and court or law enforcement officials should agree on the categories of offenses that are to be referred to them in order to eliminate minor offenses or those of no concern.

Disciplinary Reports

3-ALDF-3C-07
(Ref. 2-5309)
Written policy, procedure, and practice provide that when rule violations require formal resolution, staff members prepare a disciplinary report and forward it to the designated supervisor.

Comment:
None.

3-ALDF-3C-08
(Ref. 2-5310)
Disciplinary reports prepared by staff members include, but are not limited to, the following information:

- specific rule(s) violated
- a formal statement of the charge
- any unusual inmate behavior
- any staff witnesses
- an explanation of the event that should include who was involved, what transpired, and the time and location of occurrence
- any physical evidence and its disposition
- any immediate action taken, including the use of force
- reporting staff member's signature and date and time of report

Comment:
All relevant information should be recorded on a disciplinary report form and should be as specific and comprehensive as possible.

Section C. Rules and Discipline

Prehearing Action

3-ALDF-3C-09
(Ref. 2-5311)
Written policy, procedure, and practice specify that, when an alleged rule violation is reported, an appropriate investigation is begun within 24 hours of the time the violation is reported and is completed without unreasonable delay, unless there are exceptional circumstances for delaying the investigation.

Comment:
Investigations of alleged rule violations should begin as soon as possible after the incident is reported. The investigating officer should be a staff member but not the officer who reported the incident.

3-ALDF-3C-10
(Ref. New)
Within the disciplinary procedures document there is a provision for prehearing detention of inmates who are charged with a rule violation. The inmate's prehearing status is reviewed by the facility administrator or designee within 72 hours, including weekends and holidays.

Comment:
Prehearing detention is the confinement of an inmate in an individual cell until an investigation is completed or a hearing scheduled. Such detention should not be punitive and should be used only when necessary to ensure the inmate's safety or the security of the facility. Documentation should be provided as to the reason for detention, and no inmate should remain in prehearing detention longer than necessary.

3-ALDF-3C-11
(Ref. New)
Written policy, procedure, and practice provide that an inmate charged with a rule violation receives a written statement of the charge(s), including a description of the incident and specific rules violated. The inmate is given the statement at the same time that the disciplinary report is filed with the disciplinary committee but no less than 24 hours prior to the disciplinary hearing. The hearing may be held within 24 hours with the inmate's written consent.

Comment:
None.

3-ALDF-3C-12
(Ref. 2-5318)
Written policy and procedure provide that inmates charged with rule violations are present at the hearing, unless they waive that right in writing or through behavior. Inmates may be excluded during the testimony of any inmate whose testimony must be given in confidence. The reasons for the inmate's absence or exclusion are documented.

Comment:
None.

Disciplinary Hearing

3-ALDF-3C-13
(Ref. 2-5317)
Written policy, procedure, and practice provide that inmates charged with rule violations are scheduled for a hearing as soon as practicable but no later than seven days—excluding weekends and holidays—after the alleged violation. Inmates are notified of the time and place of the hearing at least 24 hours in advance of the hearing.

Comment:
To ensure fairness and the integrity of the disciplinary process, inmates charged with rule violations should receive hearings as soon as possible unless the hearing is prevented by exceptional circumstances, unavoidable delays, or reasonable postponements. Reasons for all delays should be documented.

3-ALDF-3C-14
(Ref. New)
Written policy, procedure, and practice provide for postponement or continuance of the disciplinary hearing for a reasonable period and good cause.

Comment:
Hearing postponement or continuance may be granted for such cause as preparation of a defense, illness or unavailability of the inmate, further investigation of factual matters relevant to the hearing, or pending criminal court prosecution. Delaying a hearing is also justifiable on the basis of factual recording of an inmate's unacceptable behavior during the hearing process or the inmate's refusal to participate in a reasonable manner.

Conduct of Hearing

3-ALDF-3C-15
(Ref. 2-5319)
Written policy, procedure, and practice provide that disciplinary hearings on rule violations are conducted by an impartial person or panel of persons. A record of the proceedings is made and maintained for at least six months.

Comment:
To ensure objectivity, hearings for rule violations should be conducted by persons who were not directly involved in the incident.

3-ALDF-3C-16
(Ref. 2-5321)
Written policy, procedure, and practice provide that inmates have an opportunity to make a statement and present documentary evidence at the hearing and can request witnesses on their behalf; the reasons for denying such a request are stated in writing.

Comment:
None.

Section C. Rules and Discipline

3-ALDF-3C-17
(Ref. 2-5320)

Written policy, procedure, and practice provide that a staff member or agency representative assist inmates at disciplinary hearings if requested. A representative is appointed when it is apparent that an inmate is not capable of collecting and presenting evidence effectively on his or her own behalf.

Comment:
Staff members or agency representatives designated to assist inmates should be trained in and knowledgeable about facility rules and discipline, disciplinary procedures, and due process requirements. Some agencies designate a legal assistant or staff representative to assist inmates in hearings. While this meets due process safeguards, an additional intent is to provide staff assistance from a person with whom inmates are comfortable and whom they feel they can trust. Therefore, inmates should be allowed to choose persons to represent them from an approved list of facility staff members. At all times, the burden is on the agency to indicate reasons for not allowing a particular staff member to represent an inmate in a specific situation.

Inmates may not cross-examine witnesses, but staff may question witnesses who have been requested by an inmate to present evidence.

3-ALDF-3C-18
(Ref. New)

Written policy, procedure, and practice provide that the disciplinary committee's decision is based solely on information obtained in the hearing process, including staff reports, the statements of the inmate charged, and evidence derived from witnesses and documents.

Comment:
Witnesses requested by the inmate may be questioned by both the inmate's representative and committee members. Witnesses who cannot respond to questions in person can be asked to submit written statements. The inmate should be permitted to obtain and submit any relevant documents.

Hearing Record

3-ALDF-3C-19
(Ref. 2-5322)

Written policy, procedure, and practice provide that a written record is made of the decision and the supporting reasons, and that a copy is given to the inmate. The hearing record and supporting documents are kept in the inmate's file and in the disciplinary committee's records.

Comment:
The disciplinary hearing record should include the decision, the disposition, and the reason for the action, unless doing so would jeopardize facility security.

3-ALDF-3C-20
(Ref. 2-5325)

Written policy, procedure, and practice provide that if an inmate is found not guilty of an alleged rule violation, the disciplinary report is removed from all of the inmate's files.

Comment:
When an inmate is found guilty of only some of the rule violations he or she was originally charged with in connection with a single incident, and when that incident is described in a single disciplinary report, the inmate's record should show clearly the violations that were not proved. All disciplinary reports, regardless of disposition, may be kept and used for statistical or research purposes providing all identification is removed.

Where there are multiple incidents, alleged rule violations for which an inmate is found not guilty must be separated and removed from the inmate's file. When multiple incidents/charges are listed on a single report, charges resulting in not-guilty findings may be marked over or blacked out.

Review

3-ALDF-3C-21
(Ref. 2-5323)

Written policy, procedure, and practice provide for review of all disciplinary hearings and dispositions by the facility administrator or designee to assure conformity with policy and regulations.

Comment:
At the conclusion of the disciplinary hearing, the hearing record should be forwarded to the facility administrator or designee for review. This review should ensure that the hearing was conducted in accordance with stated procedures and that the action taken conforms with facility regulations.

Appeal

3-ALDF-3C-22
(Ref. 2-5324)

Written policy and procedures grant inmates the right to appeal decisions of the disciplinary hearing officer(s) to the administrator or an independent authority. The administrator or independent authority either affirms or reverses the decision of the disciplinary hearing officer(s) within five days of the appeal.

Comment:
None.

Section D
Special Management

Note: "Segregation" is the generic term used to encompass administrative segregation, protective custody, and disciplinary detention. (See glossary definition.)

Principle: Inmates who threaten the secure and orderly management of the facility may be removed from the general population and placed in special units.

General Policy and Practice

3-ALDF-3D-01
(Ref. 2-5206)

Written policy, procedure, and practice govern the operation and supervision of inmates under administrative segregation, protective custody, and disciplinary detention.

Comment:
Administrative segregation: The classification committee or, in an emergency, the facility administrator may place in administrative segregation an inmate whose continued presence in the general population poses a serious threat to life, property, self, staff, or other inmates, or to the security or orderly running of the facility. Inmates in administrative segregation because of behavioral problems should be provided with programs conducive to their well-being. Inmates pending investigation for a trial on a criminal act or pending transfer can also be placed in administrative segregation; this segregation may be for relatively extensive periods of time.

Protective custody: Inmates requesting or requiring protection from the general population may be placed in protective custody. Inmates in protective custody should be allowed to participate in as many as possible of the programs afforded the general population, providing such participation does not threaten facility security. Each protective custody case should be reviewed frequently with the goal of terminating the separate housing assignment as soon as possible.

Disciplinary detention: The disciplinary committee may place inmates with serious rule violations in disciplinary detention only after an impartial hearing has determined (1) that other available alternative dispositions are inadequate to regulate the inmate's behavior within acceptable limits and (2) that the inmate's presence in the general inmate population poses a serious threat to the orderly operation or security of the facility.

Total isolation as punishment for a rule violation is not an acceptable practice; when exceptions occur, they should be justified by clear and substantiated evidence and should be fully documented.

3-ALDF-3D-02
(Ref. 2-5207)

The facility administrator or shift supervisor can order immediate segregation when it is necessary to protect the inmate or others. The action is reviewed within 72 hours by the appropriate authority.

Comment:
None.

Admission and Review of Status

3-ALDF-3D-03
(Ref. 2-5212)

Written policy, procedure, and practice provide that an inmate is admitted to protective custody status when there is documentation that protective custody is warranted and no reasonable alternatives are available.

Comment:
Protective custody should be used only for short periods of time, except when an inmate needs long-term protection and the facts are well documented. Admission to protective custody should be fully documented with a consent form signed by the inmate.

3-ALDF-3D-04
(Ref. 2-5208)

Written policy, procedure, and practice provide that an inmate is placed in disciplinary detention for a rule violation only after a hearing.

Comment:
None.

3-ALDF-3D-05
(Ref. 2-5210)

Written policy, procedure, and practice provide for a review of the status of inmates in administrative segregation and protective custody every seven days for the first two months and at least every 30 days thereafter.

Comment:
A hearing should be held to review the status of any inmate who spends more than seven continuous days in administrative segregation or protective custody to determine whether the reasons for the placement still exist.

3-ALDF-3D-06
(Ref. 2-5211)

Written policy, procedure, and practice specify the review process used to release an inmate from administrative segregation or protective custody.

Comment:
An inmate should be released by action of the appropriate authority.

3-ALDF-3D-07
(Ref. 2-5313)

There is a sanctioning schedule for rule violations. The maximum sanction for rule violations is no more than 60 days for all violations arising out of one incident. Continuous confinement for more than 30 days requires the review and approval of the facility administrator.

Comment:
The time an inmate spends in disciplinary detention should be proportionate to the offense committed and take into consideration the inmate's prior conduct, specific program needs, and other relevant factors.

Section D. Special Management

Supervision

3-ALDF-3D-08
(Ref. New)
Written policy, procedure, and practice require that all special management inmates are personally observed by a correctional officer at least every 30 minutes on an irregular schedule. Inmates who are violent or mentally disordered or who demonstrate unusual or bizarre behavior receive more frequent observation; suicidal inmates are under continuous observation.

Comment:
None.

3-ALDF-3D-09
(Ref. 2-5226)
Written policy and procedure provide that inmates in segregation receive daily visits from the chief security officer or shift supervisor, members of the program staff on request, and a qualified health care official three times per week unless medical attention is needed more frequently.

Comment:
None.

3-ALDF-3D-10
(Ref. 2-5226)
Written policy and procedure govern the selection criteria, supervision, and rotation of staff who work directly with inmates in special management units.

Comment:
Procedures should be established to supervise and evaluate the on-the-job performance of all staff who work with inmates in segregation, and there should be administrative procedures for promptly removing ineffective staff. Officers assigned to these positions should have completed their probationary period. The need for rotation should be based on the intensity of the assignment.

3-ALDF-3D-11
(Ref. 2-5225)
Written policy, procedure, and practice provide that staff operating special management units maintain a permanent log.

Comment:
The log should contain the following information for each inmate admitted to segregation: name, number, housing location, date admitted, type of infraction or reason for admission, tentative release date, and special medical or psychiatric problems or needs. The log also should be used to record all visits by officials who inspect the units or counsel the inmates, all unusual inmate behavior, and all releases.

Part Three. Institutional Operations

General Conditions of Confinement

3-ALDF-3D-12
(Ref. New)

Written policy, procedure, and practice provide that all inmates in special management units are provided prescribed medication, clothing that is not degrading, and access to basic personal items for use in their cells unless there is imminent danger that an inmate or any other inmate(s) will destroy an item or induce self-injury.

Comment:
Inmates in segregation should be provided basic items needed for personal hygiene as well as items such as eyeglasses and writing materials. Clothing should be that of the general population unless an adjustment is necessary for self-protection, such as removal of a belt to prevent a suicide attempt, and any clothing adjustment should be justified in writing by an appropriate official. If a supervisor judges that there is imminent danger an inmate will destroy an item or use it to induce self-injury, the inmate may be deprived of the item; in such cases, every effort should be made to supply a substitute for the item or to permit the inmate to use the item under the supervision of an officer.

3-ALDF-3D-13
(Ref. 2-5215)

Written policy, procedure, and practice provide that inmates in special management units have the opportunity to shave and shower at least three times per week.

Comment:
Inmates in special management units should have the opportunity to maintain an acceptable level of personal hygiene unless these procedures cause an undue security hazard. If conditions permit, the inmates should be able to shower daily.

3-ALDF-3D-14
(Ref. 2-5216)

Written policy, procedure, and practice provide that inmates in special management units receive laundry, barbering, and hair care services and are issued and exchange clothing, bedding, and linen on the same basis as inmates in the general population. Exceptions are permitted only when found necessary by the senior officer on duty; any exception is recorded in the unit log and justified in writing.

Comment:
None.

3-ALDF-3D-15
(Ref. 2-5213)

Written policy and procedure provide that whenever an inmate in segregation is deprived of any usually authorized item or activity, a report of the action is made and forwarded to the facility administrator.

Comment:
None.

Section D. Special Management

Programs and Services

3-ALDF-3D-16
(Ref. 2-5217)

Written policy, procedure, and practice provide that inmates in special management units can write and receive letters on the same basis as inmates in the general population.

Comment:
Letters should be delivered promptly. Any item rejected consistent with policy and procedure should be returned to the sender, and the inmate should be advised of the reason for the rejection.

Visiting

3-ALDF-3D-17
(Ref. 2-5218)

Written policy, procedure, and practice provide that inmates in special management units have opportunities for visitation unless there are substantial reasons for withholding such privileges.

Comment:
Every effort should be made to notify approved visitors of any restrictions on visiting; if time allows, the burden of this notification may be placed on the inmate.

Access to Legal and Reading Materials

3-ALDF-3D-18
(Ref. 2-5221)

Written policy, procedure, and practice provide that inmates in special management units have access to legal materials.

Comment:
To ensure legal rights, inmates in special management units should have access to both personal legal materials and available legal reference materials. Reasonable arrangements should be made to assist the inmates in meeting court deadlines.

3-ALDF-3D-19
(Ref. 2-5222)

Written policy, procedure, and practice provide that inmates in special management units have access to reading materials.

Comment:
Inmates in special management units should be provided a sufficient quantity of reading materials and have the opportunity to borrow reading materials from the facility's library.

Exercise Outside of Cell

3-ALDF-3D-20
(Ref. 2-5223)

Written policy, procedure, and practice provide that inmates in special management units receive a minimum of one hour of exercise per day outside their cells, five days per week, unless security or safety considerations dictate otherwise.

Comment:
Inmates in special management units should be provided with the opportunity to exercise in an area designated for this purpose, with opportunities to exercise outdoors, weather permitting, unless security or safety considerations dictate otherwise. A written record should be kept of each inmate's participation in the exercise program. Reasons for the imposition of constraints should be documented.

Part Three. Institutional Operations

Telephone Privileges

3-ALDF-3D-21 Written policy, procedure, and practice provide that inmates are allowed
(Ref. 2-5220) telephone privileges.

Comment:
This standard also applies to inmates held in disciplinary detention for more than 60 days.

3-ALDF-3D-22 Written policy and procedure provide that inmates in administrative segregation
(Ref. 2-5220) and protective custody are allowed telephone privileges.

Comment:
None.

3-ALDF-3D-23 Written policy and procedure provide that inmates in disciplinary detention are
(Ref. 2-5219) allowed limited telephone privileges consisting of telephone calls related specifically to access to the judicial process and family emergencies as determined by the facility administrator or designee.

Comment:
None.

Administrative Segregation/Protective Custody

3-ALDF-3D-24 Written policy, procedure, and practice provide that inmates in protective cus-
(Ref. 2-5224) tody have access to programs and services that include, but are not limited to, the following:

- educational services
- commissary services
- library services
- social services
- counseling services
- religious guidance
- recreational programs

Comment:
Although services and programs cannot be identical to those provided to the general population, there should be no major differences for reasons other than danger to life, health, or safety. Inmates in administrative segregation and protective custody should have the opportunity to receive treatment from professionals such as social workers, psychologists, counselors, and psychiatrists. The standard also applies to inmates held in disciplinary detention for more than 60 days.

Section E
Inmate Rights

Principle: The facility protects the safety and constitutional rights of inmates and seeks a balance between expression of individual rights and preservation of facility order.

Access to Courts

3-ALDF-3E-01
(Ref. 2-5293)

Written policy, procedure, and practice ensure the right of inmates to have access to courts.

Comment:
The right of access to the courts minimally provides that inmates have the right to present any issue, including the following: challenging the legality of their conviction or confinement; seeking redress for illegal conditions or treatment while under correctional control; pursuing remedies in connection with civil legal problems; and asserting against correctional or other government authority any other rights protected by constitutional or statutory provision or common law. Inmates seeking judicial relief are not subjected to reprisals or penalties because of the decision to seek such relief.

Access to Counsel

3-ALDF-3E-02
(Ref. 2-5294)

Written policy, procedure, and practice ensure and facilitate inmate access to counsel and assist inmates in making confidential contact with attorneys and their authorized representatives; such contact includes, but is not limited to, telephone communications, uncensored correspondence, and visits.

Comment:
Facility authorities should assist inmates in making confidential contact with attorneys and their authorized representatives; these representatives may include law students, special investigators, lay counsel, or other persons who have a legitimate connection with the legal issue being pursued. Provision should be made for visits during normal facility hours, uncensored correspondence, telephone communications, and after-hours visits requested because of special circumstances.

Access to Law Library

3-ALDF-3E-03
(Ref. 2-5295)

Written policy, procedure, and practice provide that inmates have access to legal materials if there is not adequate free legal assistance to help them with criminal, civil, and administrative legal matters.

Inmates have access to paper, typewriters or typing service, and other supplies and services related to legal matters.

Comment:
None.

Access to Programs and Services

3-ALDF-3E-04
(Ref. 2-5301,
2-5370)

Written policy, procedure, and practice provide that program access, work assignments, and administrative decisions are made without regard to inmates' race, religion, national origin, sex, handicap, or political views.

Comment:
Inmates should be assured equal opportunities to participate in all facility programs.

3-ALDF-3E-05
(Ref. 2-5370)

Should males and females be housed in the same facility, equal opportunities are provided for participation in programs and services.

Comment:
None.

3-ALDF-3E-06
(Ref. 2-5118)

When both males and females are housed in the same facility, they are provided separate sleeping quarters but equal access to all available services and programs. Neither sex is denied opportunities solely on the basis of their smaller number in the population.

Comment:
None.

Access to Media

3-ALDF-3E-07
(Ref. 2-5300)

Written policy, procedure, and practice grant inmates the right to communicate or correspond with persons or organizations, subject only to the limitations necessary to maintain order and security.

Comment:
None.

Protection from Harm

3-ALDF-3E-08
(Ref. 2-5302)
Mandatory

Written policy, procedure, and practice protect inmates from personal abuse, corporal punishment, personal injury, disease, property damage, and harassment.

Comment:
In situations where physical force or disciplinary detention is required, only the least drastic means necessary to secure order or control should be used. Special management units should be used to protect inmates from themselves or other inmates.

Protection from Unreasonable Searches

3-ALDF-3E-09
(Ref. New)
Written policy, procedure, and practice govern all searches and preservation of evidence when an inmate is suspected of a new crime. Such searches are authorized only by the facility administrator or designee unless immediate action is necessary; in such cases the facility administrator or designee is fully informed as soon as possible after the search.

Comment:
Searches directed at solving a possible new crime should include provisions for the preservation of evidence as well as the legal protection of individual rights afforded under the Fourth Amendment. Regulations should specify the circumstances and manner in which such searches are to be conducted.

Freedom in Personal Grooming

3-ALDF-3E-10
(Ref. New)
Written policy, procedure, and practice allow freedom in personal grooming except when a valid interest justifies otherwise.

Comment:
Inmates should be permitted freedom in personal grooming as long as their appearance does not conflict with the facility's requirements for safety, security, identification, and hygiene. All regulations concerning personal grooming should be the least restrictive necessary.

Grievance Procedures

3-ALDF-3E-11
(Ref. 2-5303)
There is a written inmate grievance procedure that is made available to all inmates and includes at least one level of appeal.

Comment:
A grievance procedure is an administrative means for the expression and resolution of inmate problems. The facility's grievance mechanism should include provisions for the following: written responses to all grievances, including the reasons for the decision; response within a prescribed, reasonable time limit, with special provisions for responding to emergencies; supervisory review of grievances; participation by staff and inmates in the procedure's design and operation; access by all inmates, with guarantees against reprisals; applicability over a broad range of issues; and means for resolving questions of jurisdiction.

Part Four
Institutional Services

Section A
Reception and Orientation

Principle: All incoming inmates undergo thorough screening and assessment at admission and receive thorough orientation to the facility's procedures, rules, programs, and services.

3-ALDF-4A-01 Written policies and procedures govern the admission of inmates new to the
(Ref. 2-5346) system. These procedures include at a minimum the following:

- determination that inmate is legally committed to the facility
- drug/alcohol use
- thorough search of the individual and possessions
- disposition of personal property
- shower and hair care, if necessary
- issue of clean, laundered clothing when appropriate
- photographing and fingerprinting, including notation of identifying marks or other unusual physical characteristics
- medical, dental, and mental health screening
- assignment to housing unit
- recording basic personal data and information to be used for mail and visiting list
- explanation of mail and visiting procedures
- assistance to inmates in notifying their next of kin and families of admission
- suicide screening
- assignment of registered number to the inmate
- giving written orientation materials to the inmate
- telephone calls by inmate
- assignment of a housing unit
- criminal history check

Comment:
Staff should explain the procedures being undertaken at each step in the admissions process.

3-ALDF-4A-02 Written policy, procedure, and practice govern the admission and orientation of
(Ref. 2-5343) new inmates. They are reviewed annually and updated if necessary.

Comment:
None.

Part Four. Institutional Services

3-ALDF-4A-03 Inmates are separated from the general population during the admissions
(Ref. 2-5345) process.

Comment:
None.

Personal Property

3-ALDF-4A-04 Written policy and procedure provide for a written, itemized inventory of all
(Ref. 2-5350) personal property of newly admitted inmates and secure storage of inmate
property, including money and other valuables. The inmate is given a receipt for
all property held until release.

Comment:
None.

Section B
Classification

Principle: Inmates are classified to the most appropriate level of custody and programming both on admission and on review of their status.

3-ALDF-4B-01 Written policy, procedure, and practice provide for a written inmate classification
(Ref. 2-5352) plan in terms of level of custody required, housing assignment, and participation in correctional programs. They are reviewed at least annually and updated if necessary.

Comment:
None.

3-ALDF-4B-02 The inmate classification plan specifies criteria and procedures for determining
(Ref. 2-5353) and changing the status of an inmate, including custody, transfers, and major changes in programs. The plan includes an appeals process for classification decisions.

Comment:
None.

Special Management Inmates

3-ALDF-4B-03 The facility provides for the separate management of the following categories of
(Ref. 2-5354) inmates:

- female and male inmates
- other classes of detainees (witnesses, civil inmates)
- community custody inmates (work releases, weekender, trustees)
- inmates with special problems (alcoholics, narcotics addicts, mentally disturbed persons, physically handicapped persons, persons with communicable diseases)
- inmates requiring disciplinary detention
- inmates requiring administrative segregation
- juveniles

Comment:
None.

3-ALDF-4B-04 Written policy, procedure, and practice prohibit the confinement of juveniles
(Ref. 2-5355) under the age of 18 within the facility.

Comment:
None.

Section C
Food Service

Principle: Meals are nutritionally balanced, well-planned, and prepared and served in a manner that meets established governmental health and safety codes.

Food Service Management

3-ALDF-4C-01
(Ref. 2-5233)

Food service operations are supervised by a full-time staff member who is experienced in food service management.

Comment:
The food service manager should have the resources, authority, and responsibility to provide complete food service for the facility, including three nutritionally adequate, palatable, and attractive meals a day produced under sanitary conditions and at reasonable costs. The food service manager should have a minimum of three years' experience in food service management.

Budgeting and Purchasing

3-ALDF-4C-02
(Ref. 2-5240)

Written policy, procedure, and practice specify the food service budgeting, purchasing, and accounting practices, including but not limited to the following systems:

- **food expenditure cost accounting designed to determine cost per meal per inmate**
- **estimation of food service requirements**
- **purchase of supplies at wholesale and other favorable prices and conditions, when possible**
- **determination of and responsiveness to inmate eating preferences**
- **refrigeration of food, with specific storage periods**

Comment:
None.

3-ALDF-4C-03
(Ref. 2-5239)

Written policy, procedure, and practice require that accurate records are maintained of all meals served.

Comment:
A uniform system should be established to record the number, cost, and type of meals served inmates, employees, guests, and visitors. Employees, guests, and visitors should be served the same food inmates are served. Food service records should include published menus; information on waste, food costs, and nutritional accounting; and notation of food products raised or produced in the system.

Section C. Food Service

Dietary Allowances

ALDF-4C-04
(Ref. 2-5228,
2-5229)
Mandatory

There is documentation that the facility's dietary allowances are reviewed at least annually by a qualified nutritionist or dietician to ensure that they meet the nationally recommended allowances for basic nutrition. Menu evaluations are conducted at least quarterly by facility food service supervisory staff to verify adherence to the established basic daily servings.

Comment:
Dietary allowances, as adjusted for age, sex, and activity, should meet or exceed the recommended dietary allowances published by the National Academy of Sciences. A qualified nutritionist or dietician is a person registered or eligible for registration by the American Dietetic Association or who has the documented equivalent in education, training, or experience, with evidence of relevant continuing education.

Menu Planning

3-ALDF-4C-05
(Ref. 2-5230)

Written policy, procedure, and practice require that food service staff plan menus and substantially follow the plan and that the planning and preparation of all meals take into consideration food flavor, texture, temperature, appearance, and palatability.

Comment:
All menus, including special diets, should be planned, dated, and available for review at least one week in advance. Any substitutions in the meals actually served should be noted and should be of equal nutritional value. A file of tested recipes adjusted to a yield appropriate for the facility's size should be maintained on the premises. Food should be served as soon as possible after preparation and at an appropriate temperature. Clinical diets should be approved by a qualified nutritionist or dietician and documented accordingly.

Special Diets

3-ALDF-4C-06
(Ref. 2-5231)
Mandatory

Written policy, procedure, and practice provide for special diets as prescribed by appropriate medical or dental personnel.

Comment:
Therapeutic diets should be available on medical authorization. Specific diets should be prepared and served to inmates according to the orders of the treating physician or dentist or as directed by the responsible health authority official. Medical diet prescriptions should be specific and complete, furnished in writing to the food service manager, and rewritten monthly. Special diets should be kept as simple as possible and should conform as closely as possible to the foods served other inmates.

Part Four. Institutional Services

3-ALDF-4C-07
(Ref. 2-5232)

Written policy, procedure, and practice provide for special diets for inmates whose religious beliefs require the adherence to religious dietary laws.

Comment:
Religious diets should be approved by the chaplain. Religious diet prescriptions should be specific and complete, furnished in writing to the food service manager, and rewritten monthly. Special diets should be kept as simple as possible and should conform as closely as possible to the food served other inmates.

3-ALDF-4C-08
(Ref. 2-5238)

Written policy precludes the use of food as a disciplinary measure.

Comment:
All inmates and staff except those on special medical or religious diets should eat the same meals. Food should not be withheld, nor the standard menu varied, as a disciplinary sanction for an individual inmate. The standard does not preclude rewarding groups of inmates with special food in return for special services or under special circumstances.

Health and Safety Regulations

3-ALDF-4C-09
(Ref. 2-5242)
Mandatory

There is documentation by an independent, outside source that food service facilities and equipment meet established governmental health and safety codes; corrective action is taken on deficiencies, if any.

Comment:
Food service facilities and equipment should meet all standards and requirements set by qualified professional and/or governmental bodies. Food service personnel should be trained in accident prevention, first aid, use of safety devices, floor care, knife storage, and use of fire extinguishers. They should attend regular meetings to discuss accident prevention and analyze major accidents to prevent recurrence.

3-ALDF-4C-10
(Ref. New)

Written policy, procedure, and practice provide that all staff and other persons are trained in the use of the equipment safety procedures to be followed in the food service department.

Comment:
None.

Section C. Food Service

3-ALDF-4C-11
(Ref. 2-5234)
Mandatory

Written policy, procedure, and practice provide for adequate health protection for all inmates and staff in the facility and inmates and other persons working in the food service, including the following:

1. Where required by the laws and/or regulations applicable to food service employees in the community where the facility is located, all persons involved in the preparation of food receive a preassignment medical examination and periodic reexaminations to ensure freedom from diarrhea, skin infections, and other illnesses transmissible by food or utensils; all examinations are conducted in accordance with local requirements.
2. When the facility's food services are provided by an outside agency or individual, the facility has written verification that the outside provider complies with the state and local regulations regarding food service.
3. All food handlers are instructed to wash their hands on reporting to duty and after using toilet facilities.
4. Inmates and other persons working in food service are monitored each day for health and cleanliness by the director of food services (or designee).

Comment:
All food service personnel should be in good health and free from communicable disease and open infected wounds; have clean hands and fingernails; wear hairnets or caps; wear clean, washable garments; and employ hygienic food-handling techniques. Federal facilities should apply appropriate regulations such as those of the U.S. Public Health Service.

Inspections

Food Products

3-ALDF-4C-12
(Ref. 2-5241)

When required by statute, food products that are grown or produced within the system are inspected and approved by the appropriate government agency; there is a distribution system that ensures prompt delivery of foodstuffs to facility kitchens.

Comment:
All such foodstuffs should meet or surpass government inspection levels, and the distribution system should ensure that they are delivered when fresh and in a condition for optimum food service.

Government inspection of food grown in inmate gardens and used in food service is not required where the garden is not part of a larger agriculture operation and the inmate does not work full-time at food production for use by the inmate population; all garden-grown food should, however, be inspected by food service personnel prior to use.

Part Four. Institutional Services

Facilities and Equipment

3-ALDF-4C-13
(Ref. 2-5241)
Mandatory

Written policy, procedure, and practice require weekly inspections of all food service areas, including dining and food preparation areas and equipment, by administrative, medical, or dietary personnel; these may include the person supervising food service operations or his/her designee. Refrigerator and water temperatures are checked daily by administrative, medical, or dietary personnel.

Comment:
All areas and equipment related to food preparation (e.g., ranges, ovens, refrigerators, mixers, dishwashers, garbage disposal) require frequent inspections to ensure their sanitary and operatable condition. Water temperature on the final dishwasher rinse should be 180 degrees Fahrenheit; between 140 and/or above 140 degrees Fahrenheit is appropriate if a sanitizer is used on the final rinse. The person conducting the inspection should have some training in food service operations.

3-ALDF-4C-14
(Ref. New)

Shelf goods are maintained at 45 degrees to 80 degrees Fahrenheit; refrigerated foods at 35 degrees to 40 degrees Fahrenheit; and frozen foods at 0 degrees Fahrenheit or below.

Comment:
None.

Meal Service

3-ALDF-4C-15
(Ref. 2-5236)

Written policy, procedure, and practice provide that meals are served under conditions that minimize regimentation, and with supervision by staff members.

Comment:
None.

3-ALDF-4C-16
(Ref. 2-5237)

Written policy, procedure, and practice require that at least three meals (including two hot meals) are provided at regular meal times during each 24-hour period, with no more than 14 hours between the evening meal and breakfast. Variations may be allowed based on weekend and holiday food service demands provided basic nutritional goals are met.

Comment:
When inmates are not routinely absent from the facility for work or other purposes, at least three meals should be provided at regular times during each 24-hour period.

Section D
Sanitation and Hygiene

Principle: The facility's sanitation and hygiene program complies with applicable regulations and standards of good practice to protect the health and safety of inmates and staff.

Sanitation Inspections

3-ALDF-4D-01
(Ref. 2-5243)
Mandatory Written policy, procedure, and practice require the following inspections:

- weekly sanitation inspections of all facility areas by a qualified departmental staff member
- comprehensive and thorough monthly inspections by a safety/sanitation specialist
- at least annual inspections by federal, state, and/or local sanitation and health officials or other qualified person(s)

The facility complies with all applicable laws and regulations of the governing jurisdiction, and there is documentation by an independent, outside source that any past deficiencies noted in annual inspections have been corrected.

Comment:
The safety/sanitation specialist responsible for conducting monthly inspections may be a facility staff member who is trained in the application of jurisdictional codes and regulations. Periodically and on an as-needed basis, this individual is provided assistance from specialists regarding safety and sanitation requirements and inspections. Training for this individual may be provided through the agency's central office specialist(s) or by other applicable agencies.

Water Supply

3-ALDF-4D-02
(Ref. 2-5244)
Mandatory The facility's potable water source and supply, whether owned and operated by the public water department or the facility, is certified by an independent, outside source to be in compliance with jurisdictional laws and regulations.

Comment:
None.

Waste Disposal

3-ALDF-4D-03
(Ref. 2-5248)
Mandatory There is a written plan that provides for the disposal of liquid, solid, and toxic wastes.

Comment:
None.

Part Four. Institutional Services

Housekeeping

3-ALDF-4D-04
(Ref. 2-5247)
Mandatory

There is a written plan for the control of vermin and pests that includes, at a minimum, monthly inspections by a qualified person.

Comment:
None.

3-ALDF-4D-05
(Ref. 2-5245)

A written housekeeping plan for all areas of the facility's physical plant provides for daily housekeeping and regular maintenance by assigning specific duties and responsibilities to staff and inmates.

Comment:
Effective housekeeping requires the development of a definite cleaning schedule with personnel and inmates assigned specific duties. Cleaning activities should be supervised at all times to ensure that the work performed is proper and thorough.

Clothing and Bedding Supplies

3-ALDF-4D-06
(Ref. 2-5254)

The store of clothing, linen, and bedding exceeds that required for the facility's inmate population.

Comment:
More clothing, linen, and bedding should be available than needed at any one time, so there is no delay in replacing items.

3-ALDF-4D-07
(Ref. 2-5253)

Written policy specifies accountability for inmate clothing and bedding.

Comment:
The issue of all clothing and bedding should be recorded, and inmates should be held accountable for use.

Clothing Issue

3-ALDF-4D-08
(Ref. 2-5249)

Written policy, procedure, and practice provide for the issue of suitable clothing to all inmates. Clothing is properly fitted, climatically suitable, durable, and presentable.

Comment:
A standard wardrobe should be provided at the time of admission and should include, as appropriate: shirts, blouses, dresses, trousers, skirts, belts, undergarments, slips, socks, shoes, coats, jackets, and headwear. In addition to the standard issue of inmate clothing, civilian attire should be available in limited quantities for leisure, visiting, work release, and furloughs.

3-ALDF-4D-09
(Ref. 2-5251)

Written policy, procedure, and practice provide for the issue of special and, when appropriate, protective clothing and equipment to inmates assigned to the facility's food service, hospital, farm, garage, physical plant, maintenance shops, and other special work details.

Comment:
Inmates assigned to special work areas should be clothed in accordance with the requirements of their work assignment and, when appropriate, be furnished with suitable protective equipment (disposable face masks and gloves, protective helmets, goggles).

3-ALDF-4D-10
(Ref. 2-5255)

There is provision for needed cleaning and storage of inmate personal clothing.

Comment:
None.

Bedding and Linen Issue

3-ALDF-4D-11
(Ref. 2-5252)

Written policy, procedure, and practice provide for the issue of suitable, clean bedding and linen, including two sheets, pillow and pillowcase, one mattress, and sufficient blankets to provide comfort under existing temperature controls. There is provision for linen exchange, including towels, at least weekly.

Comment:
Collection, storage, and exchange methods for bedding and linens should be done hygienically; i.e., blankets, pillows, and mattresses should be cleaned before reissue, and linen and towels must be laundered before reissue.

3-ALDF-4D-12
(Ref. 2-5256)

Written policy, procedure, and practice require that articles necessary for maintaining proper personal hygiene are provided to all inmates.

Comment:
None.

Hair Care Services

3-ALDF-4D-13
(Ref. 2-5259)

Hair care services and facilities are available to inmates.

Comment:
None.

Section E
Health Care

Principle: The facility provides comprehensive health care services by qualified personnel to protect the health and well-being of inmates.

3-ALDF-4E-01
(Ref. 2-5260)

Written policy and procedure provide for the delivery of health care services, including medical, dental, and mental health services, under the control of a designated health authority. When this authority is other than a physician, final medical judgments rest with a single designated responsible physician licensed in the state. Arrangements are made with health care specialists in advance of need.

Comment:
The parties to the agreement are the governmental funding agency responsible for the facility and/or the facility administrator and the health authority. The responsibility of the health authority includes arranging for all levels of health care and assuring quality of and inmate access to all health services.

3-ALDF-4E-02
(Ref. 2-5261)
Mandatory

Written policy, procedure, and practice provide that all medical, psychiatric, and dental matters involving medical judgment are the sole province of the responsible physician and dentist, respectively.

Comment:
The provision of health care is a joint effort of administrators and health care providers and can be achieved only through mutual trust and cooperation. The health authority arranges for the availability of health care services; the official responsible for the facility provides the administrative support for making the services accessible to inmates.

3-ALDF-4E-03
(Ref. 2-5262)

Written policy, procedure, and practice provide that the health authority meets with the facility administrator at least quarterly and submits annual statistical summaries and quarterly reports on the health care delivery system and health environment.

Comment:
Minutes of the quarterly administrative meetings may be used to meet the requirements for a quarterly report. The report should address such topics as the effectiveness of the health care system, description of any health environment factors that need improvement, changes effected since the last reporting period, and, if needed, recommended corrective action. The health authority should report immediately any condition that poses a danger to staff or inmate health and safety. The annual statistical report should indicate the number of inmates receiving health services by category of care as well as other pertinent information (e.g., operative procedures, referrals to specialists, ambulance services, etc.).

Section E. Health Care

3-ALDF-4E-04
(Ref. 2-5263)

Each policy, procedure, and program in the health care delivery system is reviewed at least annually by the appropriate health care authority and revised if necessary. Each document bears the date of the most recent review or revision and signature of the reviewer.

Comment:
None.

General Policies

Continuity of Care

3-ALDF-4E-05
(Ref. New)

Written policy, procedure, and practice require continuity of care from admission to discharge from the facility, including referral to community care when indicated.

Comment:
When health care is transferred to providers in the community, appropriate health information should be shared with the new providers in accordance with consent requirements.

Unimpeded Access to Care

3-ALDF-4E-06
(Ref. 2-5278)

Written policy and procedure require that inmates' health complaints are solicited daily, acted on by health-trained correctional personnel, and followed by appropriate triage and treatment by qualified health personnel.

Comment:
None.

Facilities and Equipment

3-ALDF-4E-07
(Ref. 2-5264)

For health care delivered in the facility, adequate space, equipment, supplies, and materials are provided as determined by the health authority.

Comment:
The type of space and equipment/treatment room will depend on the level of health care provided in the facility and the capabilities and desires of the health providers. In all facilities, space should be provided where the inmate can be examined and treated in private.

Basic equipment generally includes thermometers, blood pressure cuffs, stethoscope, ophthalmoscope, otoscope, percussion hammer, scale, examining table, gooseneck lights, wash basin, and transportation equipment (e.g., wheelchair and litter). If female inmates receive medical services in the facility, appropriate equipment should be available for pelvic examinations.

Part Four. Institutional Services

3-ALDF-4E-08
(Ref. 2-5266)

Written policy and procedure require that the facility provide 24-hour emergency medical and dental care available as outlined in a written plan, that includes provisions for the following arrangements:

- on-site emergency first aid and crisis intervention
- emergency evacuation of the inmate from the facility
- use of an emergency medical vehicle
- use of one or more designated hospital emergency rooms or other appropriate health facilities
- emergency on-call physician, dentist, and mental health professional services when the emergency health facility is not located in a nearby community
- security procedures providing for the immediate transfer of inmates when appropriate

Comment:
Arrangements should be made with nearby hospitals or other facilities for all health services that cannot be appropriately provided within the facility or where contractual arrangements can result in a better or broader range of services. In the event the usual health services are not available, particularly in emergency situations, the facility should have developed a backup to serve the program. The plan might include an alternate hospital emergency service or a physician "on call" service.

Personnel

Qualifications

3-ALDF-4E-9
(Ref. 2-5270)
Mandatory

Appropriate state and federal licensure, certification, or registration requirements and restrictions apply to personnel who provide health care services to inmates. The duties and responsibilities of such personnel are governed by written job descriptions approved by the health authority. Verification of current credentials and job descriptions are on file in the facility.

Comment:
Only qualified health care personnel should determine and supervise health care procedures. Written job descriptions should include the required professional qualifications and the individual's specific role in the health care delivery system. Verification of qualifications may consist of copies of current credentials or a letter from the state licensing or certifying body regarding current credential status. Nursing services are performed in accordance with professionally recognized standards of nursing practice and the jurisdiction's Nurse Practice Act.

Section E. Health Care

Administration of Treatment

3-ALDF-4E-10
Mandatory
Written policy, procedure, and practice provide that all treatment by health care personnel other than a physician, dentist, psychologist, optometrist, podiatrist, or other independent provider is performed pursuant to written standing or direct orders by personnel authorized by law to give such orders. Nurse practitioners and physician's assistants may practice within the limits of applicable laws and regulations.

Comment:
Standing medical orders are orders written for the definitive treatment of identified conditions and for the on-site emergency treatment of any person having such a condition. Direct orders are those written specifically for the treatment of one person's particular condition.

Mental Health Services

3-ALDF-4E-11
(Ref. New)
Written policy, procedure, and practice specify the provision of mental health services for inmates. These services include but are not limited to those provided by qualified mental health professionals who meet the educational and license/certification criteria specified by their respective professional disciplines (e.g., psychiatric nursing, psychiatry, psychology, and social work).

Comment:
An adequate number of qualified staff members should be available to deal directly with inmates who have severe mental health problems as well as to advise other correctional staff in their contacts with such individuals.

3-ALDF-4E-12
(Ref. New)
Written policy, procedure, and practice, approved by the appropriate mental health authority, provide for all activities carried out by mental health service personnel.

Comment:
The goal of mental health services is to provide for the detection, diagnosis, treatment, and referral of inmates with mental health problems and to provide a supportive environment during all stages of each inmate's period of incarceration.

Health-trained Staff Member

3-ALDF-4E-13
(Ref. 2-5267)
In facilities without full-time, qualified health personnel, a health-trained staff member coordinates the health care delivery in the facility under the joint supervision of the responsible health authority and facility administrator.

Comment:
None.

3-ALDF-4E-14
(Ref. 2-5268)
The health authority systematically determines health care personnel requirements in order to provide inmate access to health care staff and services.

Comment:
None.

Adult Local Detention Facilities, Third Edition

Students and Interns

3-ALDF-4E-15
(Ref. New)
Written policy, procedure, and practice provide that any students or interns delivering health care in the facility work under direct staff supervision, commensurate with their level of training.

Comment:
The direct staff supervision may be provided by a physician, nurse, or other appropriate health care personnel.

Inmate Assistants

3-ALDF-4E-16
(Ref. 2-5272)
Written policy, procedure, and practice provide that inmates are not used for the following duties:

- **performing direct patient care services**
- **scheduling health care appointments**
- **determining access of other inmates to health care services**
- **handling or having access to surgical instruments, syringes, needles, medications, or health records**
- **operating diagnostic or therapeutic equipment**

Comment:
Inmates cannot operate medical equipment but should be able to perform maintenance and housekeeping services under close supervision of qualified staff. In addition, inmates participating in a certified vocational training program may perform direct services, such as dental chairside assistance.

Section E. Health Care

Pharmaceuticals

3-ALDF-4E-17
(Ref. 2-5288)
Mandatory

Written policy, procedure, and practice provide for the proper management of pharmaceuticals and address the following subjects:

- a formulary specifically developed for the facility
- prescription practices, including requirements that (1) psychotropic medications are prescribed only when clinically indicated as one facet of a program of therapy; (2) "stop order" time periods are required for all medications; and (3) the prescribing provider reevaluates a prescription prior to its renewal
- procedures for medication receipt, storage, dispensing, and administration or distribution
- maximum security storage and periodic inventory of all controlled substances, syringes, and needles
- dispensing of medicine in conformance with appropriate federal and state law
- administration of medication by persons properly trained and under the supervision of the health authority and facility administrator or designee
- accountability for administering or distributing medications in a timely manner, according to physician orders

Comment:
The written formulary lists should include all prescribed and nonprescribed medications stocked in the facility or generated by outside health care providers. Any dispensed medication (one or more doses issued from a stock or bulk container) should be labeled with the patient's name, prescription contents, directions for use, and other vital information. The pharmacy may be managed by a resident pharmacist or by health-trained personnel under the supervision of the health authority.

3-ALDF-4E-18
(Ref. New)

Psychotropic drugs, such as antipsychotics, antidepressants, and drugs requiring parenteral administration, are prescribed only by a physician or authorized health provider by agreement with the physician, and then only following a physical examination of the inmate by the health provider. Such drugs are administered by the responsible physician, qualified health personnel, or health-trained personnel under the direction of the health authority.

Comment:
None.

Part Four. Institutional Services

Health Screenings and Examinations

Preliminary Screening

3-ALDF-4E-19
(Ref. 2-5273)
Mandatory

Written policy, procedure, and practice require medical, dental, and mental health screening to be performed by health-trained or qualified health care personnel on all inmates, excluding intrasystem transfers, on the inmate's arrival at the facility. All findings are recorded on a form approved by the health authority. The screening includes at least the following:

Inquiry into:

- current illness and health problems, including venereal diseases and other infectious diseases
- dental problems
- mental health problems
- use of alcohol and other drugs, including type(s) of drugs used, mode of use, amounts used, frequency used, date or time of last use, and history of any problems that may have occurred after ceasing use (e.g., convulsions)
- past and present treatment or hospitalization for mental disturbance or suicide
- possibility of pregnancy
- other health problems designated by the responsible physician

Observation of:
-
- behavior, including state of consciousness, mental status, appearance, conduct, tremor, and sweating
- body deformities, ease of movement, etc.
- condition of skin, including trauma markings, bruises, lesions, jaundice, rashes and infestations, and needle marks or other indications of drug abuse

Medical disposition of inmate:
-
- general population OR
- general population with prompt referral to appropriate health care service OR
- referral to appropriate health care service for emergency treatment

---

Comment:
Health screening is a system of structured inquiry and observation designed to (1) prevent newly arrived inmates who pose a health or safety threat to themselves or others from being admitted to the general population and (2) rapidly transport newly admitted inmates to needed health care. Receiving screening can be performed by health care personnel or by a health-trained correctional officer at the time of admission. Facilities that have reception and diagnostic units and/or a holding room must conduct receiving screening on all inmates on arrival at the facility as part of the admission procedures.

**3-ALDF-4E-20
(Ref. 2-4290)
Mandatory**

Written policy, procedure, and practice require that all intrasystem transfers receive a health screening by health-trained or qualified health care person immediately on arrival at the facility. All findings are recorded on a screening form approved by the health authority. The screening includes at a minimum the following:

Inquiry into:

- whether the inmate is being treated for a medical, dental, or mental problem
- whether the inmate is presently on medication
- whether the inmate has a current medical, dental, or mental health complaint

Observation of:

- general appearance and behavior
- physical deformities, evidence of abuse and/or trauma

Medical disposition of inmate:

- general population OR
- general population with appropriate referral to health care service OR
- referral to appropriate health service for emergency treatment

Comment:
Health screening of intrasystem transfers is necessary to detect inmates who pose a health or safety threat to themselves or others and who may require immediate health care.

3-ALDF-4E-21
(Ref. 2-5274)
Mandatory

Written policy, procedure, and practice require that health appraisal for each inmate, excluding intrasystem transfers, is completed within 14 days after arrival at the facility. If there is documented evidence of a health appraisal within the previous 90 days, a new health appraisal is not required except as determined by the designated health authority. Health appraisal includes the following:

- review of the earlier receiving screening
- collection of additional data to complete the medical, dental, mental health, and immunization histories
- laboratory and/or diagnostic tests to detect communicable disease, including venereal disease and tuberculosis
- recording of height, weight, pulse, blood pressure, and temperature
- other tests and examinations as appropriate
- medical examination, including review of mental and dental status
- review of the results of the medical examination, tests, and identification of problems by a physician or other qualified health care personnel, if such is authorized in the medical practice act
- initiation of therapy when appropriate
- development and implementation of treatment plan, including recommendations concerning housing, job assignment, and program participation

Comment:
Test results, particularly for communicable diseases, should be received and evaluated before an inmate is assigned to housing in the general population. Information regarding the inmate's physical and mental status also may dictate housing and activity assignments. When appropriate, additional investigation should be conducted into alcohol and drug abuse and other related problems. A routine appraisal by mental health staff should be completed within 30 days of admission on all new inmates.

3-ALDF-4E-22
(Ref. New)

Written policy, procedure, and practice for the collection and recording of health appraisal data require the following:

1. The process is completed in a uniform manner as determined by the health authority.
2. Health history and vital signs are collected by health-trained or qualified health personnel.
3. Collection of all other health appraisal data is performed only by qualified health personnel.

Comment:
None.

Section E. Health Care

Dental Screening and Examination

3-ALDF-4E-23
(Ref. 2-5277)

Written policy and procedure require that dental care is provided to each inmate under the direction and supervision of a dentist, licensed in the state, as follows:

- dental screening within 14 days of admission
- dental hygiene services within 14 days of admission
- dental examinations within three months of admission
- dental treatment, not limited to extractions, within three months of admission when the health of the inmate would be adversely affected

Comment:
None.

Levels of Care

Emergency Care

3-ALDF-4E-24
(Ref. 2-5271)
Mandatory

Written policy, procedure, and practice provide that correctional and other personnel are trained to respond to health-related situations within a four-minute response time. The training program is established by the responsible health authority in cooperation with the facility administrator and includes the following:

- recognition of signs and symptoms and knowledge of action required in potential emergency situations
- administration of first aid and cardiopulmonary resuscitation (CPR)
- methods of obtaining assistance
- signs and symptoms of mental illness, retardation, and chemical dependency
- procedures for patient transfers to appropriate medical facilities or health care providers

Comment:
The required CPR certification must be current at the time of the audit, consistent with jurisdictional statutes for certification. The preferred minimum CPR course covers mouth-to-mouth breathing, one- and two-rescuer CPR care for conscious or unconscious choking victims, and respiratory emergencies.

First Aid

3-ALDF-4E-25
(Ref. 2-5265)

First aid kits are available in designated areas of the facility based on need.

Comment:
The availability and placement of first aid kits are determined by the designated health authority in conjunction with the facility administrator. The health authority approves the contents, number, location, and procedures for monthly inspection of the kit(s) and develops written procedure for the use of the kits by nonmedical staff.

Part Four. Institutional Services

Sick Call

3-ALDF-4E-26
(Ref. 2-5279)

Written policy, procedure, and practice require that sick call is conducted by a physician and/or other qualified personnel and is available to all inmates. Sick call is available as follows:

1. Facilities with fewer than 100 inmates hold sick call one day per week, at a minimum.
2. Facilities with 100 to 300 inmates hold sick call three days per week, at a minimum.
3. Facilities with more than 300 inmates hold sick call four days per week, at a minimum.

If an inmate's custody status precludes attendance at sick call, arrangements are made to provide sick call services in the place of the inmate's detention.

Comment:
Sick call is defined as the system through which an inmate reports and receives individualized and appropriate medical services for nonemergency illness or injury.

Use of Specialists

3-ALDF-4E-27
(Ref. New)

Arrangements are made with health care specialists in advance of need.

Comment:
An inmate's illness may require the services of a specialist at any time; therefore, arrangements should be made with appropriate consultants in advance of need.

3-ALDF-4E-28
(Ref. 2-5280)

Written policy and procedure require that arrangements are made for the provision of special medical programs, including chronic care, convalescent care, and medical preventive maintenance for the inmates.

Comment:
None.

Prostheses and Orthodontic Devices

3-ALDF-4E-29
(Ref. 2-5282)

Written policy and procedure require that, as determined by the responsible physician or dentist, medical and dental prostheses are provided when the health of the inmate would otherwise be adversely affected.

Comment:
None.

Section E. Health Care

Transfer for Needed Care

3-ALDF-4E-30
(Ref. New)

Written policy, procedure, and practice require that patients who need health care beyond the resources available in the facility, as determined by the responsible physician, are transferred under appropriate security provisions to a facility where such care is available.

Comment:
Treatment of an inmate's health problem should not be limited by the resources and services available within the facility. Health care staff should cooperate with security personnel in determining conditions of transportation and necessary security precautions when an inmate needs to be transported to another facility or clinic.

3-ALDF-4E-31
(Ref. New)

Written policy, procedure, and practice provide that prior to transfer to another facility or other substantial travel, either the inmates or their records are evaluated by health care personnel to assess suitability for travel.

When travel is approved, pertinent data (including medication, behavior management procedures, and other treatment or special requirements for observation and care during travel) are documented in a manner readily accessible to and easily understood by transportation staff or others who may be called upon to attend inmates during travel and on reception at the receiving facility. Medications or other special treatment required enroute, along with specific written instructions for administration, are furnished to transportation staff.

Comment:
Full health coverage should be provided for all inmate transfers. Although the emphasis during transportation must be on security, the medical, dental, and mental health aspects should not be overlooked.

Use of Restraints

3-ALDF-4E-32
(Ref. 2-5283)

Written policy and procedure govern the use of restraints for medical and psychiatric purposes.

Comment:
Where restraints are part of a health care treatment regimen, the restraints used should be those that would be appropriate for the general public within the jurisdiction. Written policy should identify the authorization needed and when, where, and how restraints may be used and for how long.

Part Four. Institutional Services

Specialized Programs

Health Education

3-ALDF-4E-33
(Ref. New)

Written policy, procedure, and practice provide that a program of health eduction is provided to inmates of the facility.

Comment:
Health education includes information on medical services and immunizations; personal hygiene; dental hygiene; nutrition; venereal disease, tuberculosis, and other communicable diseases; effects of smoking; self-examination for breast cancer; substance abuse; dangers of self-medication; hypertension detection; family planning, including appropriate services and referrals; physical fitness; and self-care for chronic diseases and/or disabilities.

Suicide Prevention and Intervention

3-ALDF-4E-34
(Ref. 2-5271-1)

There is a written suicide prevention and intervention program that is reviewed and approved by a qualified medical or mental health professional. All staff with responsibility for inmate supervision are trained in the implementation of the program.

Comment:
The program should include specific procedures for intake screening, identification, and supervision of suicide-prone inmates.

Serious and Infectious Disease

3-ALDF-4E-35
(Ref. 2-5263-1)

Written policy, procedure, and practice address the management of serious and infectious diseases. These are updated as new information becomes available.

Comment:
Because of their serious nature, methods of transmission, and public sensitivity, infectious diseases such as tuberculosis, hepatitis-B, and AIDS (acquired immunodeficiency syndrome) require special attention. Agencies should work with the responsible health authority in establishing policy and procedure that include the following: an ongoing education program for staff and inmates; control, treatment, and prevention strategies, that may include screening and testing, special supervision and/or special housing arrangements, as appropriate; protection of individual confidentiality; and media relations.

Section E. Health Care

3-ALDF-4E-36
(Ref. 2-5263-2)
There are written policies and procedures that specify approved actions to be taken by employees concerning inmates who have been diagnosed as HIV positive. This policy is reviewed annually and includes, at a minimum, the following:

- when and where inmates are to be tested
- appropriate safeguards for staff and inmates
- who shall conduct the tests
- when and under what conditions inmates are to be separated from the general population
- medical referrals required
- staff and inmate training procedures
- issues of confidentiality

Comment:
None.

Severe Mental Illness and Retardation

3-ALDF-4E-37
(Ref. 2-5275)
Written policy and procedure require postadmission screening and referral for care of mentally ill or retarded inmates whose adaptation to the correctional environment is significantly impaired.

Comment:
None.

3-ALDF-4E-38
(Ref. 2-5276)
Written policy requires consultation between the facility administrator and the responsible physician or their designees under the following conditions before the following actions are taken regarding patients who are diagnosed as having a psychiatric illness:

- housing assignments
- program assignments
- disciplinary measures
- transfers in and out of the facility

Comment:
None.

Detoxification

3-ALDF-4E-39
(Ref. 2-5281)
Written policy and procedure provide that detoxification at the facility is done under medical supervision.

Comment:
None.

Part Four. Institutional Services

3-ALDF-4E-40
(Ref. 2-5371)

The facility provides counseling and program services for inmates with drug and alcohol addiction problems.

Comment:
Alcoholics and drug addicts pose special problems for facility staff. During the withdrawal or "drying out" process, medical care may be necessary which requires prior arrangements with a nearby medical facility. Organizations such as Alcoholics Anonymous and Narcotics Anonymous can be helpful in providing a wide range of services for addicts, and increasingly, community substance abuse treatment programs have been bringing their services to detention facilities.

Management of Chemical Dependency

3-ALDF-4E-41
(Ref. 2-5281, 2-5371)

Written policy and procedure guide the clinical management of chemically dependent inmates and include the following requirements:

- diagnosis of chemical dependency
- determination as to whether an individual requires nonpharmacologically or pharmacologically supported care
- individualized treatment plans developed and implemented by a multidisciplinary team
- referrals to specified community resources on release, when appropriate
-

Comment:
None.

Informed Consent

3-ALDF-4E-42
(Ref. 2-5284)

All examinations, treatments, and procedures affected by informed consent standards in the community are likewise observed for inmate care. In the case of minors, the informed consent of parent, guardian, or legal custodian applies when required by law. Health care is rendered against an inmate's will only in accordance with law.

Comment:
None.

Inmate Participation in Research

3-ALDF-4E-43
(Ref. 2-5285)
Mandatory

Written policy and practice prohibit the use of inmates for medical, pharmaceutical, or cosmetic experiments. This policy does not preclude individual treatment of an inmate based on his or her need for a specific medical procedure that is not generally available.

Comment:
None.

Section E. Health Care

Notification of Designated Individuals

3-ALDF-4E-44
(Ref. 2-5286)

Written policy and procedure specify and govern the process by which the individuals designated by the inmate are notified in case of serious illness or injury. If possible, permission for notification is obtained from the inmate prior to need.

Comment:
The persons to be notified should be designated in writing as part of the facility's admissions procedures. Whenever possible, the facility should obtain the inmate's consent prior to notifying any designated individuals.

Inmate Death

3-ALDF-4E-45
(Ref. 2-5287)

Written policy and procedure specify and govern the actions to be taken in the event of an inmate's death.

Comment:
The medical examiner or coroner should be notified of the inmate's death immediately. A postmortem examination should be performed if the cause of death is unknown; if the death occurred under suspicious circumstances; or if the inmate was not under current medical care.

Health Record Files

Contents

3-ALDF-4E-46
(Ref. 2-5290)

The health record file contains the following items:

- completed admission screening form
- health appraisal data forms
- all findings, diagnoses, treatments, dispositions
- record of prescribed medications and their administration
- laboratory, x-ray, and diagnostic studies
- signature and title of documenter
- consent and refusal forms
- release-of-information forms
- place, date, and time of health encounters
- health service reports, e.g., dental, mental health, and consultations
- treatment plan, including nursing care plan
- progress reports
- discharge summary of hospitalization and other termination summaries

The method of recording entries in the records, the form and format of the records, and the procedures for their maintenance and safekeeping are approved by the health authority.

Comment:
All findings, including notations concerning mental health, dental, and consultative services, should be recorded at the time of service delivery or no later than 14 days from the time of discharge or termination of treatment. The receiving screening form should become a part of the record at the time of the first health encounter.

Part Four. Institutional Services

Confidentiality

3-ALDF-4E-47
(Ref. 2-5291)

Written policy and procedure govern the confidentiality of the health record and require that, at a minimum:

1. The active health record is maintained separately from the confinement record.
2. Access to the health record is controlled by the health authority.
3. The health authority shares with the facility administrator information regarding an inmate's medical, management, security and ability to participate in programs.

Comment:
None.

Transferred and Inactive Records

3-ALDF-4E-48
(Ref. 2-5292)

Written policy, procedure, and practice regarding the transfer of health records and information establish the following requirements:

1. Summaries or copies of the health record are routinely sent to the facility to which the inmate is transferred.
2. Written authorization by the inmate is necessary for transfer of health record and information unless otherwise provided by law or administrative regulation having the force and effect of law.
3. Health record information is also transmitted to specific and designated physicians or medical facilities in the community upon the written authorization of the inmate.

Comment:
None.

Section F
Social Services

Principle: The facility makes available the professional services necessary to meet the identified needs of inmates. Such services may include individual and family counseling, family planning and parent education, and programs for inmates with drug and alcohol addiction problems.

3-ALDF-4F-01
(Ref. 2-5367)

Written policy and procedure provide that inmate programs and services are available and include, but are not limited to, social services, religious services, recreation, and leisure time activities.

Comment:
None.

3-ALDF-4F-02
(Ref. 2-5368)

The plan for inmate programs and services provides for the identification and use of available community resources.

Comment:
None.

Counseling

3-ALDF-4F-03
(Ref. 2-5371)

Written policy, procedure, and practice provide that staff are available to counsel inmates on request; provision is made for counseling and crisis intervention services.

Comment:
Staff members should make time available, on a regularly scheduled basis, for appointments with inmates who request them. Treatment offerings should include group therapy and group and individual counseling. Because inmates may have problems that require immediate attention, at least one staff member should be available 24 hours a day. Crisis intervention services should be available on an as-needed basis to assist disturbed inmates.

Counseling for Pregnant Inmates

3-ALDF-4F-04
(Ref. New)

Written policy, procedure, and practice require that comprehensive counseling and assistance are provided to pregnant inmates in keeping with their expressed desires in planning for their unborn children.

Comment:
Counseling and social services should be available from either facility staff or community agencies to assist inmates in making decisions such as whether to keep their child, give the child up for adoption, or consent to an abortion. The written policy and defined procedures should be developed based on a formal legal opinion.

Substance Abuse Programs

3-ALDF-4F-05 **Written policy, procedure, and practice provide for substance abuse programs**
(Ref. 2-5371) **for inmates with drug and alcohol addiction problems.**

Comment:
These programs should include the following:

- staff trained in drug and alcohol treatment to design and supervise the program
- selection and training of former addicts and recovering alcoholics to serve as employees or volunteers in these programs
- coordination with community substance abuse programs
- efforts to motivate addicts to seek help
- realistic goals for the rehabilitation of inmates with substance abuse problems
- a variety of approaches to provide flexibility to meet the varying needs of different addicts

Section G
Release

Principle: The facility provides a structured program to help inmates make a satisfactory transition on their release from incarceration.

Release Preparation

3-ALDF-4G-01 A program of release preparation is available to all inmates to prepare them for
(Ref. 2-5379) release from the facility.

Comment:
None.

3-ALDF-4G-02 When the facility is designated to operate any type of pretrial intervention service
(Ref. 2-5026) or other release program, its authority and responsibility are stated by statute or
administrative regulation.

Comment:
None.

3-ALDF-4G-03 When a pretrial intervention program, diversion program, pretrial release pro-
(Ref. 2-5378) gram, or parole program is conducted in the facility, sufficient staff, space, and
equipment are provided to service the program.

Comment:
None.

Temporary and Graduated Release

3-ALDF-4G-04 Temporary release programs are required to have the following elements:
(Ref. 2-5382)

- written operational procedures
- careful screening and selection procedures
- written rules of inmate conduct
- a system of supervision
- a system for evaluating program effectiveness
- efforts to obtain community cooperation and support

Comment:
None.

3-ALDF-4G-05 Where statute permits, written policy and procedure allow for inmate participa-
(Ref. 2-5381) tion in work or educational release programs.

Comment:
None.

Part Four. Institutional Services

3-ALDF-4G-06
(Ref. 2-5380)
Where statute permits, written policy and procedure allow inmates escorted and unescorted leaves into the community.

Comment:
None.

Final Release

3-ALDF-4G-07
(Ref. 2-5351)
Written procedures for releasing inmates at the end of their term include, but are not limited to, the following:

- **verification of identity**
- **verification of release papers**
- **completion of release arrangements, including notification of the parole authorities in the jurisdiction of release, if required**
- **return of personal effects or contraband**
- **verification that no facility property leaves the facility**
- **arrangements for completion of any pending action, such as grievances or claims for damages or lost possessions**
- **medical screening and arrangements for community follow-up where needed**
- **instructions on forwarding of mail**

Comment:
The release process should ensure that all matters relating to the facility are completed. If released to another agency or facility, everyone involved should understand what is to occur with respect to timing, expectations, forwarding of records, and responsibility for completing the transfer.

Part Five
Inmate Programs

Section A
Work and Correctional Industries

Principle: A written body of policy and procedure governs the facility's work programs for inmates, including correctional industries. Policy and procedure address federal, state, and local regulations, the inmate workday, and compensation for work performed.

Inmate Work Plan

3-ALDF-5A-01
(Ref. 2-5357)

The facility has a written inmate work assignment plan that provides for inmate employment, subject to the number of work opportunities available and the maintenance of facility security.

Comment:
None.

3-ALDF-5A-02
(Ref. 2-5369)

Written policy, procedure, and practice can require all able-bodied inmates to work unless assigned to an approved education or training program. Inmates have the option of refusing to participate in a rehabilitation or treatment program except adult basic education and programs required by statute or ordered by the sentencing court or paroling authority.

Comment:
All able-bodied inmates are expected to participate in work assignments, adult basic education programs, and programs ordered by the sentencing court or paroling authority or required by statute. Failure to participate in programs may result in administrative action.

3-ALDF-5A-03
(Ref. 2-5363)

The inmate work plan includes provision for employment for handicapped inmates.

Comment:
None.

3-ALDF-5A-04
(Ref. 2-5362)

Written policy and procedure prohibit discrimination in inmate work assignments based on sex, race, religion, and national origin.

Comment:
None.

Part Five. Inmate Programs

3-ALDF-5A-05
(Ref. 2-5358)

Written policy provides that pretrial and unsentenced detainees are not required to work except to do personal housekeeping. Any inmate may volunteer for work assignments or facility programs.

Comment:
None.

Work Opportunities

3-ALDF-5A-06
(Ref. New)

The facility provides a variety of work assignments that afford inmates an opportunity to learn job skills and develop good work habits and attitudes that they can apply to jobs after they are released.

Comment:
Whenever possible, inmates should gain work experience relevant to the current job market; assignments for female inmates should expand beyond the traditional tasks assigned to women.

3-ALDF-5A-07
(Ref. 2-5359, 2-5360, 2-5361)

The facility provides opportunities for inmate employment in correctional industries, facility maintenance, operations, and, to the extent possible, public works and community projects.

Comment:
Many necessary jobs related to maintenance and facility operations can be done by inmates. Inmates may be assigned to construction work, conservation projects, or other work financed by public funds. These programs may be housed separately from the main facility. Staff supervising such inmates should be trained for such an assignment.

3-ALDF-5A-08
(Ref. 2-5359)

The inmate work plan includes provision for work in facility maintenance and operation.

Comment:
None.

3-ALDF-5A-09
(Ref. 2-5360)

Where statute permits, the inmate work plan provides for inmate work assignment in public works projects.

Comment:
None.

3-ALDF-5A-10
(Ref. 2-5361)

Where statute permits, the inmate work plan includes provision for inmates to work in various nonprofit and community service projects.

Comment:
None.

Section A. Work and Correctional Industries

3-ALDF-5A-11
(Ref. New)
Written policy, procedure, and practice provide that the staff operating inmate work programs use the advice and assistance of labor, business, and industrial organizations to assist in providing skills relevant to the job market.

Comment:
The facility should actively pursue cooperation from labor and industry to help plan and evaluate its work programs and assist in work release, job training, and job placement. The establishment of advisory boards or joint councils should be considered.

3-ALDF-5A-12
(Ref. New)
Written policy, procedure, and practice provide that the inmate workday approximates the workday in the community.

Comment:
None.

Work, Health, and Safety Standards

3-ALDF-5A-13
(Ref. 2-5365)
Mandatory
Inmate working conditions comply with all applicable federal, state, or local work safety laws and regulations.

Comment:
None.

Correctional Industries

3-ALDF-5A-14
(Ref. New)
There is a statute and/or written policy and procedure that authorizes the establishment of an industries program and delineates the areas of authority, responsibility, and accountability for the program.

Comment:
Effective administration of an industries program results from carefully formulated constitutional, legislative, and/or policy definition. The legal and/or operational framework of the program must be clearly established as the basis for assessing the program's performance and identifying needed changes. The role of the agency's industries administrator should be clearly defined in relation to that of the facility administrator, who is responsible for all facility programs and activities.

3-ALDF-5A-15
(Ref. New)
Written policy, procedure, and practice provide that the number of inmates assigned to industries operations meet the realistic workload needs of each industries operating unit.

Comment:
To ensure that realistic working conditions prevail, the industries management should determine the number of workers necessary to handle the workload. Job descriptions outlining responsibilities and performance expectations should be available for each job.

Part Five. Inmate Programs

3-ALDF-5A-16
(Ref. New)
Each industries operating unit has a written quality control procedure that provides for raw material, in-process, and final product inspection.

Comment:
Quality control plans should include product specifications and tolerances or dimensions as well as production techniques, along with the use of appropriate measures for determining conformance to those standards. The plans should also stress periodic inspections throughout the entire production process—including inspection of the finished product—whether such inspections are of a random or statistical sampling or of all products made. Quality control records should be maintained and used for training purposes.

3-ALDF-5A-17
(Ref. New)
A cost accounting system for each operating industries unit is designed, implemented, and maintained in accordance with generally accepted accounting principles.

Comment:
The cost accounting system should be based on a chart of accounts and general ledger that generate data for other fiscal reports. The system should include a means for recording and allocating the direct and indirect costs and the administrative overhead for each operating unit.

Inmate Compensation

3-ALDF-5A-18
(Ref. 2-5364)
Written policy and procedure require that inmates are compensated for work performed. Incentives such as monetary compensation, special housing, extra privileges, and good-time credits should be distributed according to written guidelines.

Comment:
Inmates should be compensated so that they can make purchases from the canteen and accumulate funds to assist them on their release from detention.

3-ALDF-5A-19
(Ref. 2-5366)
Where statute permits, the inmate work plan includes provision for earning credits toward a reduction in sentence.

Comment:
None.

Section B
Academic and Vocational Education

Principle: A written body of policy and procedure governs the facility's academic and vocational education program for inmates, including program accreditation, staff certification, and coordination with other facility programs and services as well as the community.

Comprehensive Education Program

3-ALDF-5B-01 Written policy and procedure provide for inmate access to educational programs,
(Ref. 2-5375) vocational counseling and, when available, vocational training.

Comment:
None.

3-ALDF-5B-02 The plan for inmate programs and services provides for the identification and
(Ref. 2-5368) use of available community resources.

Comment:
None.

Section C
Recreation and Activities

Principle: A written body of policy and procedure governs the facility's recreation and activities programs for inmates, including program coordination and supervision, facilities and equipment, community interaction, and activities initiated by inmates.

Comprehensive Recreational Program

3-ALDF-5C-01
(Ref. 2-5375)

Written policy and procedure provide inmates with access to recreational opportunities and equipment, including one hour daily of physical exercise outside the cell, and outdoors when weather permits.

Comment:
None.

Equipment and Facilities

3-ALDF-5C-02
(Ref. 2-5373)

Written policy and procedure provide opportunities for all inmates to participate in leisure time activities outside the cell or room on a daily basis.

Comment:
None.

Section D
Mail, Telephone, Visiting

Principle: A written body of policy and procedure governs the facility's mail, telephone, and visiting service for inmates, including mail inspection, public phone use, and routine and special visits.

Mail

Inmate Correspondence

3-ALDF-5D-01
(Ref. 2-5327)
Written policy and procedure govern inmate correspondence; they are available to all staff and inmates, reviewed annually and updated as needed.

Comment:
None.

3-ALDF-5D-02
(Ref. 2-5328)
When the inmate bears the mailing cost, there is no limit on the volume of letters he/she can send or receive or on the length, language, content, or source of mail or publications, except when there is reasonable belief that limitation is necessary to protect public safety or facility order and security.

Comment:
The number of approved correspondents for an inmate should be unlimited, and there should be no limit on the number of letters an inmate may send or receive from approved correspondents. Limits may be placed on use of mail for the conduct of an inmate business.

3-ALDF-5D-03
(Ref. 2-5329)
Written policy, procedure, and practice provide that indigent inmates, as defined in policy, receive a specified postage allowance to maintain community ties.

Comment:
An inmate without financial resources should be provided the means to send a reasonable number of letters per month. Community ties include family, personal friends, etc., but not privileged communication to attorneys, public officials, and courts.

Access to Publications

3-ALDF-5D-04
(Ref. 2-5330)
Written policy and procedure govern inmate access to publications.

Comment:
Policy and procedure should define which publications are allowed in the facility and how they will be inspected. Restriction to access should be related directly to maintenance of facility order and security.

Part Five. Inmate Programs

Inspection of Letters and Packages

3-ALDF-5D-05
(Ref. 2-5332)
Written policy, procedure, and practice provide that inmate mail, both incoming and outgoing, may be opened and inspected for contraband. Mail is read, censored, or rejected when based on legitimate facility interests of order and security. Inmates are notified when incoming or outgoing letters are withheld in part or in full.

Comment:
Case law has defined legal limits on censorship of mail. Inmates should be permitted uncensored correspondence so long as the correspondence poses no threat to the safety and security of the facility, public officials, or the general public and is not being used to further illegal activities. When inmate mail is censored or rejected, the inmate or author should be notified of the reasons for the action and have an opportunity to appeal that decision; such appeals should be referred to officials who did not participate in the original disapproval of the correspondence.

3-ALDF-5D-06
(Ref. 2-5334)
Written policy, procedure, and practice specify that inmates are permitted to send sealed letters to a specified class of persons and organizations, including but not limited to the following: courts; counsel; officials of the confining authority; state and local chief executive officers; administrators of grievance systems; and members of the paroling authority. Mail to inmates from this specified class of persons and organizations may be opened only to inspect for contraband and only in the presence of the inmate, unless waived in writing.

Comment:
None.

3-ALDF-5D-07
(Ref. 2-5333)
Written policy and procedure provide for the inspection of inmate letters and packages to intercept cash, checks, money orders, and contraband. A receipt is given the addressee.

Comment:
None.

3-ALDF-5D-08
(Ref. 2-5331)
Written policy, procedure, and practice require that, excluding weekends and holidays, incoming and outgoing letters are held for no more than 24 hours and packages are held for no more than 48 hours.

Comment:
Inspection for contraband in letters should take no longer than 24 hours to complete so that incoming letters should be distributed to inmates and outgoing letters sent to the post office within 24 hours of receipt. Similarly, inspection of packages should take no longer than 48 hours to complete. The standard does not prohibit the holding of mail for inmates who are temporarily absent from the facility (e.g., hospital, court).

Section D. Mail, Telephone, Visiting

Telephone

3-ALDF-5D-09
(Ref. 2-5335) **Written policy, procedure, and practice provide for inmate access to telephones.**

Comment:
Telephone facilities should permit reasonable and equitable access to all inmates and permit a reasonable amount of privacy. Procedures should specify the hours during which the telephone is available, the maximum length of calls, and any limitation on calls. All long-distance calls should be made collect.

Visiting

3-ALDF-5D-10
(Ref. 2-5337) **Written policy, procedure, and practice provide that the number of visitors an inmate may receive and the length of visits may be limited only by the facility's schedule, space, and personnel constraints or when there are substantial reasons to justify such limitations.**

Comment:
Inmates should not be denied access to visits with persons of their choice except when the facility administrator or designee can present clear and convincing evidence that such visitation jeopardizes the safety and security of the facility or the visitors.

3-ALDF-5D-11
(Ref. 2-5340) **Written policy and procedure govern visiting for high risk inmates.**

Comment:
None.

Extended and Special Visits

3-ALDF-5D-12
(Ref. 2-5341) **Written policy and procedure govern special visits.**

Comment:
None.

3-ALDF-5D-13
(Ref. New) **Where statute permits, written policy, procedure, and practice provide for extended visits between inmates and their families.**

Comment:
Policy and procedure should provide specific guidelines for determining which inmates are permitted extended visits with family; the length of the visit; where the visit should take place; and other conditions. Inmates with appropriate security classifications should be permitted furloughs home of up to three days. Also, if permitted by statute, the facility should provide suitable private accommodations on facility grounds for extended visits between inmates and their families.

Part Five. Inmate Programs

3-ALDF-5D-14
(Ref. New)
Where statute permits, written policy, procedure, and practice provide that inmates with appropriate security classifications are allowed furloughs to the community to maintain community and family ties, seek employment opportunities, and for other purposes consistent with the public interest.

Comment:
Unescorted leaves of absence for a set period of time may be appropriate to allow inmates to participate in work and study release programs, make residential plans for parole, or any other purpose consistent with the inmate's security classification.

Visitor Registration

3-ALDF-5D-15
(Ref. 2-5338)
Written policy, procedure, and practice provide that visitors register on entry into the facility and specify the circumstances under which visitors may be searched.

Comment:
Each visitor should register his or her name, address, and relation to the inmate. Staff may search visitors and their belongings according to written procedure.

3-ALDF-5D-16
(Ref. New)
The facility provides information to visitors about transportation to the facility and facilitates transportation between the facility and nearby public transit terminals.

Comment:
Facilities situated considerable distances from public transit terminals should try to provide transportation for visitors, particularly when transportation costs are significant.

Section E
Library

Principle: A written body of policy and procedure governs the facility's library program, including acquisition of materials, hours of availability, and staffing.

Comprehensive Library Services

3-ALDF-5E-01
(Ref. 2-5376)
Library services are available to all inmates in detention facilities and, at a minimum, reading materials are available to inmates in holding units.

Comment:
Library services provided should include, at a minimum: materials responsive to the interests and educational needs of users; information service to locate facts needed; programs for individuals or group information and enjoyment, such as books, media, discussion groups, music, creative writing, and speakers; and a distinct library setting.

Library materials should include up-to-date informational, recreational, legal, and educational resources appropriate to individual inmates both in the library and in the living units, including segregation units. Library resources should be supplemented by the entire collection of local, regional, and state libraries; law libraries; and interlibrary loan services. When appropriate, the resources of the libraries for the blind and physically handicapped should be used.

3-ALDF-5E-02
(Ref. 2-5377)
The facility has a qualified staff person who coordinates and supervises library services.

Comment:
This position may be full-time or part-time and may be filled by volunteer or contract personnel. If the person is not a trained librarian, he/she should receive training in library services.

Selection and Acquisition of Materials

3-ALDF-5E-03
(Ref. New)
Written policy defines the principles, purposes, and criteria used in selection and maintenance of library materials.

Comment:
Library materials should be selected to meet the educational, informational, and recreational needs of the inmates. They should be easily accessible and regulated by a system that prevents abuse.

3-ALDF-5E-04
(Ref. 2-5376)
The library participates in interlibrary loan programs when available.

Comment:
Participation in interlibrary loan programs with local and state public library systems can increase the materials available to inmates without increasing acquisition expenses.

Section F
Religious Programs

Principle: A written body of policy and procedure governs the facility's religious programs for inmates, including program coordination and supervision, opportunities to practice the requirements of one's faith, and use of community resources.

Program Coordination and Supervision

3-ALDF-5F-01
(Ref. 2-5298-1)

There is a chaplain(s) with two minimum qualifications of (1) Clinical Pastoral Education or equivalent specialized training and (2) endorsement by the appropriate religious certifying body.

Comment:
The chaplain shall assure equal status and protection for all religions.

3-ALDF-5F-02
(Ref. 2-5298-2)

In facilities with an average daily population of 500 or more inmates there is a full-time chaplain(s). For facilities with less than 500 inmates adequate religious staffing is available.

Comment:
None.

3-ALDF-5F-03
(Ref. 2-5298-3)

The chaplain(s) in cooperation with the facility administrator (and/or his designee) plans, directs, and supervises all aspects of the religious program, including approval and training of both lay and clergy volunteers from faiths represented by the inmate population. The chaplain (s) has access physically to all areas of the facility to minister to inmates and staff.

Comment:
The religious program shall be designed to fulfill the responsibility of the facility to ensure that all inmates are able to voluntarily exercise their constitutional right to religious freedom.

3-ALDF-5F-04
(Ref. New)

The chaplain has physical access to all areas of the facility to minister to inmates and staff.

Comment:
None.

3-ALDF-5F-05
(Ref. New)

The chaplain or designated religious staff member develops and maintains close relationships with community religious resources.

Comment:
Community resources can help augment the delivery of appropriate religious services on special holidays or as needed to meet the requirements of the diversity of religious faiths among inmates.

Section F. Religious Programs

Opportunity to Practice One's Faith

3-ALDF-5F-06
(Ref. 2-5372)
Written policy, procedure, and practice provide that inmates have the opportunity to participate in practices of their religious faith that are deemed essential by the faith's judicatory, limited only by documentation showing threat to the safety of persons involved in such activity or that the activity itself disrupts order in the facility.

Comment:
Religious practices include, but are not limited to, access to religious publications; religious symbols; congregate worship/religious services in appropriate space; individual and group counseling; religious study classes; and adherence to dietary requirements. Inmates in administrative segregation are allowed to participate in such religious practices subject to the same limitations stated in the standard.

In determining what constitutes legitimate religious practices, the facility administrator or designee should consider whether there is a body of literature stating religious principles that support the practices and whether the practices are recognized by a group of people who share common ethical, moral, or intellectual views.

3-ALDF-5F-07
(Ref. 2-5298-4)
When a religious leader of an inmate's faith is not represented through the chaplaincy staff or volunteers, the chaplain(s) assists the inmate in contacting such a person. That person shall have the appropriate credentials from the faith judicatory and may minister to the inmate under the supervision of the chaplain.

Comment:
The religious leader may visit at designated regular times, with provision for emergency visits.

3-ALDF-5F-08
(Ref. 2-5298)
Written policy, procedure, and practice provide that inmates have the opportunity to participate in practices of their religious faith that are deemed essential by the faith's judicatory, limited only by documentation showing threat to the safety of persons involved in such activity or that the activity itself disrupts order in the facility.

Comment:
Religious practices shall include, but are not limited to: access to religious publications; religious symbols; congregate worship/religious services in appropriate space; individual and group counseling; religious study classes; and adherence to dietary requirements. Inmates in administrative segregation shall be allowed to participate in such religious practices subject to the same limitations. In determining what constitutes legitimate religious practices, the facility administrator or designee should consider whether there is a body of literature stating religious principles that support the practices and whether the practices are recognized by a group of people who share common ethical, moral, or intellectual views.

Part Five. Inmate Programs

Religious Facilities and Equipment

3-ALDF-5F-09
Ref. 2-5298-5)

Written policy, procedure, and practice require that the facility provides space and equipment adequate for the conduct and administration of religious programs. The facility provides for the availability of noninmate clerical staff for confidential material.

Comment:
Sufficient space shall be available for congregate worship/religious services, individual counseling, group counseling and/or religious studies, and chaplaincy offices. Equipment, office supplies, and secretarial help shall be adequate to meet the needs of the religious program. Volunteers are acceptable as clerical support staff.

3-ALDF-5F-10
(Ref. 2-5298-6)

The chaplain(s), in cooperation with the facility administrator or designee, develops and maintains communications with faith communities and approves donations of equipment or materials for use in religious programs.

Comment:
The approval of such donations will ensure equipment and materials for the approved religious practices, as well as avoid accumulation of duplicate or inappropriate materials.

Appendix A
Definition of "Qualified Individual" for Safety and Sanitation Inspections

Several standards refer to documentation and inspections by "qualified individuals." (For example, Building and Safety Codes (2A), Fire Safety (3B), Food Service (4C), Sanitation and Hygiene (4D), and Work and Correctional Industries (5A) standards.) Such persons may also be referred to as "independent, qualified source," "qualified departmental staff member," "qualified designee," or "qualified fire and safety officer."

A "qualified individual" is a person whose training, education, and/or experience specifically qualifies him or her to do the job indicated in the standard.

I. General Requirements

When a standard calls for inspections, the individual conducting them needs to be trained in the application of appropriate codes and regulations. Standards do not specify the number of hours of training required, as this is determined in part by the tasks assigned. At a minimum, though, the qualified individual must (1) be familiar with the applicable codes and regulations and their requirements; (2) be able to use the appropriate instruments for measuring and documenting code compliance; (3) be able to complete checklists and prepare the necessary reports; and (4) have the authority to make corrections when deficiencies are found.

Training is often obtained from code officials or inspectors (fire marshals, building officials); government agencies that have statutory authority for inspections in a particular area (health department, labor department); or private organizations, such as the National Fire Protection Association. Often the individual obtains written certification or approval from these authorities to conduct in-house inspections. When trained and certified by the above sources to do so, a central office specialist may train and assist facility staff to conduct inspections.

II. Specific Requirements

A. Authority Having Jurisdiction

The term "authority having jurisdiction" is defined as follows:

> The authority having jurisdiction may be a federal, state, local, or other regional department or individual, such as the fire chief, fire marshal, chief of a fire prevention bureau, labor department, health department, building official, electrical inspector, or others with statutory authority. The authority having jurisdiction may be employed by the department/agency, provided that he or she is not under the authority of the facility administrator and that the report generated is referred to higher authorities within the department/agency independent of influence by the facility administrator or staff. This rule applies no matter who generates the report.

The definition also applies to the terms "independent, qualified source" and "independent, outside source."

B. Inspections

Qualified individuals conducting the monthly and weekly inspections required in the standards may be institutional staff members.

The qualified individual responsible for conducting *monthly* inspections (e.g., fire and safety officer, safety/sanitation specialist) may be an institutional staff member trained in the application of jurisdictional codes and regulations. Periodically and as needed, this individual receives assistance from the independent

Appendix A

authority or central office specialist(s) on requirements and inspections. This assistance may include participation in quarterly or biannual inspections. Training for the individual conducting the monthly inspections may be provided by the applicable agencies or through the agency's central office specialist(s).

The qualified departmental staff member who conducts *weekly* inspections of the facility may be an institutional staff member who has received training in and is familiar with the safety and sanitation requirements of the jurisdiction. At a minimum, on-the-job training from the facility's safety/sanitation specialist or the fire and safety officer regarding applicable regulations is expected, including use of checklists and methods of documentation.

The periodic weekly and monthly inspections may be conducted by either a combination of qualified individuals or one specialist, as long as the schedules and minimum qualifications described above are met. Safety and sanitation inspections may be conducted by the same person, provided this individual is familiar with the regulations for both types of inspections. When safety and sanitation requirements differ substantially, it may sometimes be necessary to call on several qualified individuals to conduct the inspections required by the standards. Using more than one person is strongly recommended.

III. Compliance Audits

In conducting standards compliance audits, Commission Visiting Committees will review documentation submitted by the facilities to assist them in judging the qualifications of these individuals. In making compliance decisions, the audit teams will look closely at the facility's entire program—both practices and results—for ensuring safety and sanitation.

Appendix B
Guidelines for the Control and Use of Flammable, Toxic, and Caustic Substances

This appendix provides definitions and recommendations to assist agencies in the application of standards that address the control of materials that present a hazard to staff and inmates.

Substances that do not contain any of the properties discussed in the guidelines but are labeled "Keep out of reach of children" or "May be harmful if swallowed" are not necessarily subject to the controls specified in the guidelines. Their use and control, however, including the quantities available, should be evaluated and addressed in agency policy. Questions concerning the use and control of any substance should be resolved by examining the manufacturer's Material Safety Data Sheet.

I. Definitions

Flash point—The minimum temperature at which a liquid will give off sufficient vapors to form an ignitable mixture with the air near the surface of the liquid (or in the vessel used).

Flammable liquid—A substance with a flash point below 100 degrees Fahrenheit (37.8 degrees Centigrade). Classified by flash point as a Class I liquid. (See Table B.)

Combustible liquid—A substance with a flash point at or above 100 degrees Fahrenheit. Classified by flash point as a Class II or Class III liquid. (See Table B.)

Toxic material—A substance that, through chemical reaction or mixture, can produce possible injury or harm to the body by entry through the skin, digestive tract, or respiratory tract. The toxicity is dependent on the quantity absorbed and the rate, method, and site of absorption. (See Table B.)

Caustic material—A substance capable of destroying or eating away by chemical reaction. (See Table B.)

It is possible that a substance may possess more than one of the above properties; therefore the safety requirements for all applicable properties should be considered.

II. General Guidelines

A. Issuance

All flammable, caustic, and toxic substances should be issued (i.e., drawn from supply points to canisters or dispensed) only under the supervision of authorized staff.

B. Amounts

All such substances should be issued only in the amount necessary for one day's needs.

C. Supervision

All persons using such substances should be closely supervised by qualified staff.

D. Accountability

All such substances must be accounted for before, during, and after their use.

Table B
Common Flammable, Toxic, and Caustic Substances

Class I Liquids
Gasoline
Benzine (Petroleum ether)
Acetone
Hexane
Lacquer
Lacquer thinner
Denatured alcohol
Ethyl alcohol
Xylene (Xylol)
Contact cement (flammable)
Toludi (Toluene)
Methyl ethyl ether
Methyl ethyl ketone
Naphtha Y, M, and P

Class II Liquids
Diesel fuel
Motor oil
Kerosene
Cleaning solvents
Mineral spirits
Agitene

Class III Liquids
Paints (oil base)
Linseed oil
Mineral oil
Neatsfoot oil
Sunray conditioner
Guardian fluid

Toxic Substances
Ammonia
Chlorine
Antifreeze
Duplicating fluid
Methyl alcohol
Defoliants
Herbicides
Pesticides

Caustic Substances
Lye
Muriatic acid
Caustic soda
Sulfuric acid
Tannic acid

Appendix B

III. Specific Guidelines for Storage, Use, and Disposal

A. Flammable and Combustible Liquids

Any liquid or aerosol that is required to be labeled "Flammable" or "Combustible" under the Federal Hazardous Substances Labeling Act must be stored and used according to label recommendations and in a way that does not endanger life and property.

1. Storage

Lighting fixtures and electrical equipment in flammable liquid storage rooms must conform to the *National Electrical Code* requirements for installation in hazardous locations.

Storage rooms must meet the following specifications:

- Be of fire-resistant construction and properly secured.
- Have self-closing fire doors at all openings.
- Have either a four-inch sill or a four-inch depressed floor (inside storage rooms only).
- Have a ventilation system—either mechanical or gravity flow within twelve inches of the floor—that provides at least six air changes per hour in the room.

Each storage cabinet must be

- Properly constructed and securely locked.
- Conspicuously labeled "Flammable—Keep Fire Away."
- Used to store no more than sixty gallons of Class I or Class II liquids or 120 gallons of Class III liquids.

Storage rooms and cabinets must be properly secured and supervised by an authorized staff member any time they are in use. Doors and cabinets shall be placed so that they do not obstruct access to exits, stairways, and other areas normally used for evacuation in the event of fire or other emergency.

All portable containers for flammable and combustible liquids other than the original shipping containers must be approved safety cans listed or labeled by a nationally recognized testing laboratory. Containers should bear legible labels identifying the contents.

All excess liquids should remain in their original container in the storage room or cabinet. All containers should be tightly closed when not in use.

2. Use

The use of any flammable or combustible liquid must conform with the provisions and precautions listed in the manufacturer's Material Safety Data Sheet.

Flammable and combustible liquids can be dispensed only by an authorized staff member. The only acceptable methods for drawing from or transferring these liquids into containers inside a building are (1) through a closed piping system; (2) from safety cans; (3) by a device drawing through the top; or (4) by gravity through an approved self-closing system. An approved grounding and bonding system must be used when liquids are dispensed from drums.

Only liquids with a flash point at or above 100 degrees Fahrenheit (e.g., Stoddard solvents, kerosene) can be used for cleaning. Such operations must be performed in an approved parts cleaner or dip-tank fitted with a fusible link lid with a 160 degree F melting-temperature link. *Under no circumstances can flammable liquids be used for cleaning.*

Appendix B

3. Disposal

Excess flammable or combustible liquids must be disposed of properly. The Material Safety Data Sheet for each substance prescribes the proper method of disposal and related precautions.

4. Spills

Information on the proper course of action for chemical spills is contained in the Material Safety Data Sheet for each substance.

B. Toxic and Caustic Substances

1. Storage

All toxic and caustic materials are to be stored in their original containers in a secure area in each department. The manufacturer's label must be kept intact on the container.

2. Use

Toxic and caustic substances can be drawn only by a staff member. The Material Safety Data Sheet for each substance details the necessary provisions and precautions for its use.

Unused portions are to be returned to the original container in the storage area or, if appropriate, stored in the storage area in a suitable, clearly labeled container.

3. Disposal

See disposal guidelines for Flammable and Combustible Liquids above.

4. Spills

See spills guidelines for Flammable and Combustible Liquids above.

C. Poisonous Substances

Poisonous substances or chemicals are those that pose a very high (Class I) caustic hazard due to their toxicity. Examples: methyl alcohol; sulfuric acid; muriatic acid; caustic soda; tannic acid. There are special precautions on the control and use of methyl alcohol (also known as wood alcohol or methanol), which is a flammable, poisonous liquid commonly used in industrial applications (e.g., shellac thinner, paint solvent, duplicating fluid, solvents for leather cements and dyes, flushing fluid for hydraulic brake systems). *Drinking methyl alcohol can cause death or permanent blindness.*

The use of any product containing methyl alcohol must be directly supervised by staff. Products containing methyl alcohol in a diluted state, such as shoe dye, may be issued to inmates or residents, but only in the smallest workable quantities.

Immediate medical attention is imperative whenever methyl alcohol poisoning is suspected.

D. Other Toxic Substances

1. Permanent antifreeze containing ethylene glycol should be stored in a locked area and dispensed only by authorized staff.

2. Typewriter cleaner containing carbon tetrachloride or tricholorochane should be dispensed in small quantities and used under direct supervision.

3. The use of cleaning fluid containing carbon tetrachloride or tetrachloride or tricholoroethylene must be strictly controlled.

Appendix B

4. Glues of all types may contain hazardous chemicals and should receive close attention at every stage of handling. Nontoxic products should be used when possible. Toxic glues must be stored under lock and used under close supervision.

5. The use of dyes and cements for leather requires close supervision. Nonflammable types should be used whenever possible.

6. Ethyl alcohol, isopropyl alcohol, and other antiseptic products should be stored and used only in the medical department. The use of such chemicals must be closely supervised. Whenever possible, such chemicals should be diluted and issued only in small quantities so as to prevent any injurious or lethal accumulation.

7. Pesticides contain many types of poisons. The staff member with responsibility for the facility's safety program should be responsible for purchasing, storing, and dispensing any pesticide. All pesticides should be stored under lock. NOTE: Only chemicals approved by the Environmental Protection Agency shall be used. DDT and 1080 (sodium fluoracetate) are among those chemicals absolutely prohibited.

8. Herbicides must be stored under lock. The staff member responsible for herbicides must have a current state license as a Certified Private Applicator. Proper clothing and protective gear must be used when applying herbicides.

9. Lyes must be used only in dye solutions and only under the direct supervision of staff.

IV. Responsibilities

A. Inventories

Constant inventories should be maintained for all flammable, toxic, and caustic substances used and stored in each department. A bin record card should be maintained for each such substance to accurately reflect acquisitions, disbursements, and the amounts on hand.

B. Departmental Files

Each department using any flammable, toxic, or caustic substance should maintain a file of the manufacturer's Material Safety Data Sheet for each substance. This file should be updated at least annually. The file should also contain a list of all areas where these substances are stored, along with a plant diagram and legend. A copy of all information in the file, including the Material Safety Data Sheets, should be supplied to the staff member responsible for the facility's safety program.

C. Master Index

The person responsible for the facility's safety program should compile a master index of all flammable, caustic, and toxic substances in the facility, including their locations and Material Safety Data Sheets. This information should be kept in the safety office (or comparable location) and should be supplied to the local fire department. The master index should also contain an up-to-date list of emergency phone numbers (e.g., local fire department, local poison control center).

D. Personal Responsibility

It is the responsibility of each person using these substances to follow all prescribed safety precautions, wear personal protective equipment when necessary, and report all hazards or spills to the proper authority. The protection of life, property, and our environment depends on it.

GLOSSARY

Adjudicatory hearing—A hearing to determine whether the allegations of a petition are supported by the evidence beyond a reasonable doubt or by the preponderance of the evidence.

Administrative segregation—A unit housing inmates whose continued presence in the general population poses a serious threat to life, property, self, staff, or other inmates.

Administrator of field services—The individual directly responsible for directing and controlling the operations of the adult probation and/or parole field services program. This person may be a division head in a large correctional agency, a chief probation officer answering to a judge, or the administrative officer of a court or parole authority with responsibility for the field services program.

Admission—The process of entry into a program. During admission processing the juvenile or adult offender receives an orientation to program goals, rules, and regulations. Assignment to living quarters and to appropriate staff is also completed at this time.

Adult community residential service—Also referred to as a halfway house, a community-based program providing a group residence (such as a house, work release center, prerelease center) for probationers, parolees, residents in incarcerated status, and referrals through the courts or other agencies. Clients may also receive these services from the agency on a nonresidential basis. (See *Out-client*.)

Adult correctional institution—A confinement facility, usually under state or federal auspices, that has custodial authority over adults sentenced to confinement for more than a year.

Adult detention facility or Jail—A local confinement facility with temporary custodial authority. Adults can be confined pending adjudication for forty-eight hours or more and usually for sentences of up to two years.

Affirmative action—A concept designed to ensure equal opportunity for all persons regardless of race, religion, age, sex, or ethnic origin. These equal opportunities include all personnel programming, such as selection, retention, rate of pay, demotion, transfer, layoff, termination, and promotion.

Aftercare—Control, supervision, and care exercised over juveniles released from facilities through a stated release process. (See *Releasing authority*.)

Agency—The unit of a governing authority that has direct responsibility for the operation of a corrections program, including the implementation of policy as set by the governing authority. For a community residential center, this would be the administrative headquarters of the facilities. A single community facility that is not part of a formal consolidation of community facilities is considered to be an agency. In a public agency, this could be a probation department, welfare department, or similar agency. For a juvenile correctional organization, this would be the central office responsible for governing the juvenile correctional system for the jurisdiction.

Agency administrator—The administrative officer appointed by the governing authority or designee who is responsible for all operations of the agency, such as the department of corrections or parole, and all related programs under his or her control.

Agency industries administrator—The individual who has functional responsibility for industries operations throughout the correctional system. Titles such as head of industries, superintendent, chief, director, or general manager may be used to denote this position.

Alternative meal—Food and/or meals that are prepared and served as an alternate to the regular meal. The alternate meal must be nutritionally adequate to ensure good health.

Audit—An examination of agency or facility records or accounts to check their accuracy, which is conducted by a person or persons not directly involved in the creation and maintenance of these records or accounts. An independent audit results in an opinion that either affirms or disaffirms the accuracy of records or accounts. An operational or internal audit usually results in a report to management that is not shared with those outside the agency.

Authority having jurisdiction—The organization or individual designated by statute, regulation, administrative rule or policy that is responsible for a specified activity, function, or operation within a correctional setting.

Booking—Both a law enforcement process and a detention facility procedure. As a police administrative action, it is an official recording of an arrest and the identification of the person, place, time, arresting authority, and reason for the arrest. In a detention facility, it is a procedure for the admission of a person charged with or convicted of an offense, and includes searching, fingerprinting, photographing, medical screening, and collecting personal history data. Booking also includes the inventory and storage of the individual's personal property.

Budget—A plan for allocation of anticipated revenues and expenditures.

Building code—Federal, state, or local regulations that dictate the construction of a facility.

Camp—A nonsecure residential program located in a relatively remote area. The residents participate in a structured program that emphasizes outdoor work, including conservation and related activities. There are often twenty to sixty residents in these facilities.

Canteen/Commissary—An area or system where approved items are available for purchase by inmates/juveniles.

Career development plan—The planned sequence of promotions within an agency that contains provision for (1) vertical movement throughout the entire range of a particular discipline, (2) horizontal movement encouraging lateral and promotional movement between disciplines, and (3) opportunity for all to compete for the position of head of the agency. Progression along these three dimensions can occur as long as the candidate has the ambition, ability, and required qualifications.

Case conference—A conference between individuals working with the juvenile or adult offender to see that court-ordered services are being provided.

Case record—Information concerning an offender's criminal, personal and medical history, behavior, and activities while in custody. The record typically includes commitment papers, court orders, detainers, personal property receipts, visitor lists, photographs, fingerprints, type of custody, disciplinary infractions and action taken, grievance reports, work assignments, program participation, and miscellaneous correspondence.

Casework—The function of the caseworker, social worker, or other professional in providing social services, such as counseling, to individuals in custody.

Cellblock—A group or cluster of single and/or multiple occupancy cells or detention rooms immediately adjacent and directly accessible to a day or activity room. In some facilities the cellblock consists of a row of cells fronted by a dayroom of corridor-like proportions.

Chemical agent—An active substance, such as tear gas, used to deter activities that might cause personal injury or property damage.

Chief of police—A local law enforcement official who is the appointed or elected chief executive of a police department and is responsible for the operation of the city jail or lockup.

Chronic care—Health care provided to patients over a long period of time.

Citizen volunteer—An individual who donates his or her time and effort to enhance the activities and programs of the agency. They are selected on the basis of their skills and personal qualities to provide services in recreation, counseling, education, religion, etc.

Classification—A process for determining the needs and requirements of those for whom confinement has been ordered and for assigning them to housing units and programs according to their needs and existing resources.

Classroom—An area specifically designed and equipped for the conduct of educational and vocational programming.

Co-correctional facility—An institution designed to house both male and female juvenile or adult offenders.

Code of ethics—A set of rules describing acceptable standards of conduct for all employees.

Commissary/Canteen—An area or system where approved items are available for purchase by inmates.

Committing authority—The agency or court responsible for placing a youth in a program.

Community resources—Human service agencies, service clubs, citizen interest groups, self-help groups, and individual citizen volunteers that offer services, facilities, or other functions that can meet the needs of the facility or have the potential to assist residents. These various resources, which may be public or private, national or local, may assist with material and financial support, guidance, counseling, and supportive services.

Glossary

Contact visiting—A program inside and/or outside the facility that permits inmates/juveniles to visit with designated person(s). The area is free of obstacles or barriers that prohibit physical contact.

Contraband—Any item possessed by confined juvenile or adult offenders or found within the facility that is illegal by law or expressly prohibited by those legally charged with the administration and operation of the facility or program.

Contractor—A person or organization that agrees to furnish materials or to perform services for the facility or jurisdiction at a specified price. Contractors operating in correctional facilities are subject to all applicable rules and regulations for the facility.

Contractual arrangement—An agreement with a private party (such as an incorporated agency or married couple) to provide services to juvenile or adult offenders for remuneration. (See Independent operator.)

Control center—The central point within a facility or institution where security activities are monitored and controlled. The control center is constructed at a level appropriate to the security level of the facility.

Corporal punishment—Any act of inflicting punishment directly on the body, causing pain or injury.

Correctional facility—A facility used for the incarceration of individuals accused or convicted of criminal activity. A correctional facility is managed by a single chief executive officer with broad authority for the operation of the facility. This authorization typically includes the final authority for decisions concerning (1) the employment or termination of staff members, and (2) the facility operation and programming within guidelines established by the parent agency or governing body.

A correctional facility must also have (1) a separate perimeter that precludes the regular commingling of the inmates with inmates from other facilities, (2) a separate facility budget managed by a chief executive officer within guidelines established by the parent agency or governing authority, and (3) staff that are permanently assigned to the facility.

Counseling—Planned use of interpersonal relationships to promote social adjustment.

County parole—The status of a county jail inmate who, convicted of a misdemeanor and conditionally released from a confinement facility prior to the expiration of sentence, has been placed under supervision in the community for a period of time.

Criminal record check—Conducted in accordance with state and federal statutes to detect any criminal convictions of an individual.

Dayroom—Space for activities that is situated immediately adjacent to the inmate/juvenile sleeping areas and separated from them by a wall.

dBA scale—A system for measuring the relative loudness of sound.

Delinquent act—An act that, if committed by an adult, would be considered a crime.

Delinquent youth—Also referred to as a juvenile delinquent or a criminal-type offender, a youth who has been charged with or adjudicated for conduct that would, under the law of the jurisdiction in which the offense was committed, be a crime if committed by an adult. (See *Status offender* and *Juvenile*.)

Detainee—Any person confined in a local detention facility not serving a sentence for a criminal offense.

Detainer—A warrant placed against a person in a federal, state, or local correctional facility that notifies the holding authority of the intention of another jurisdiction to take custody of that individual when he or she is released.

Dental screening—Conducted on initial intake with instructions on dental hygiene under the direction and supervision of a dentist with appropriate state or federal licensure.

Detention warrant—A warrant that authorizes the arrest and temporary detention of a parolee pending preliminary revocation proceedings. A detention warrant should be distinguished from a warrant for the return of a parolee to prison, although return warrants are sometimes used as detainers. For the purpose of these standards, return warrants used as detainers are also deemed to be detention warrants.

Detoxification—The process by which an individual is gradually withdrawn from a drug or alcohol addiction.

Disciplinary detention—A unit housing inmates convicted of serious rule violations.

Disciplinary hearing—A nonjudicial administrative procedure to determine if substantial evidence exists to find an inmate guilty of a rule violation.

Disciplinary report—A written report, prepared by a person with appropriate authority, describing an alleged violation of a facility's rules or regulations.

Dispositional hearing—A hearing held subsequent to the adjudicatory hearing in order to determine what order of disposition (e.g., probation, training school, foster home) should be made concerning a juvenile adjudicated as delinquent.

Diversion—The official halting or suspension, at any legally prescribed point after a recorded justice system entry, of formal criminal or juvenile justice proceedings against an alleged offender. The suspension of proceedings may be in conjunction with a referral of that person to a treatment or care program administered by a nonjudicial or a private agency, or there may be no referral.

Due process safeguards—Those procedures that ensure just, equal, and lawful treatment of an individual involved in all stages of the juvenile or criminal justice system, such as a notice of allegations, impartial and objective fact finding, the right to counsel, a written record of proceedings, a statement of any disposition ordered with the reasons for it, and the right to confront accusers, call witnesses, and present evidence.

Educational program—A program of formal academic education or a vocational training activity designed to improve employment capability.

Educational release—The designated time when residents or inmates leave the program or institution to attend school in the community, returning to custody after school hours.

Elective surgery—Surgery designed to correct a substantial functional deficit.

Emergency—Any significant disruption of normal facility or agency procedure, policy, or activity caused by riot, escape, fire, natural disaster, employee action, or other serious incident.

Emergency care—Care for an acute illness or unexpected health care need that cannot be deferred until the next scheduled sick call. Emergency care shall be provided to the resident population by the medical director, physician, or other staff, local ambulance services, and/or outside hospital emergency rooms. This care shall be expedited by following specific written procedures for medical emergencies described in the standards.

Emergency plans—Written documents that address specific actions to be taken in an institutional emergency or catastrophe such as a fire, flood, riot or other major disruption.

Emergency power—An alternate power system that is activated when the primary source of electricity is interrupted. The system may be an emergency generator, battery operated power pack, or an alternate supply source.

Environmental health—All conditions, circumstances, and surrounding influences that affect the health of individuals or groups in the area.

Facility—A place, institution, building (or part thereof), set of buildings, or area (whether or not enclosing a building or set of buildings) that is used for the lawful custody and/or treatment of individuals. It may be owned and/or operated by public or private agencies and includes the staff and services as well as the buildings and grounds.

Facility administrator—Any official, regardless of local title (e.g., sheriff, chief of police, administrator, warden/superintendent) who has the ultimate responsibility for managing and operating the facility.

Field agency—The unit of a governing authority that has direct responsibility for the provision of field supervision services and for the carrying out of policy as set by the governing authority.

Field services—Services provided to delinquent youth, status offenders, or adult offenders in the community by probation, parole, or other agencies.

Field staff—The professionals assigned case responsibility for control, supervision, and provision of program services to delinquent youth or adult offenders. (Sometimes referred to as field workers.)

Firearm—Any weapon capable of firing shots or bullets.

Fire code—Federal, state, or local regulations governing fire safety.

Glossary

First aid—Care for a condition that requires immediate assistance from an individual trained in first aid care and the use of the facility's first aid kits.

Fiscal position control—The process that ensures that individuals on the payroll are legally employed, positions are authorized in the budget, and funds are available.

Footcandle—A unit for measuring the intensity of illumination, defined as the amount of light thrown on a surface one foot away from the light source.

Force, use of—Physical force used in instances of justifiable self-defense, protection of others, protection of property, or prevention of escapes. Physical force is used only as a last resort and in accordance with appropriate statutory authority.

Formulary—A book containing a list of medicinal substances and formulas.

Furlough—A period of time during which an offender is allowed to leave the program or institution and go into the community unsupervised for various purposes consistent with public interest.

Good-time—A system established by law whereby a convicted offender is credited a set amount of time, which is subtracted from his or her sentence, for specified periods of time served in an acceptable manner.

Governing authority—In public/governmental agencies, the administrative department or division to which the agency reports; the policy-setting body. In private agencies, this may be an administrative headquarters, central unit, or the board of directors or trustees.

Grievance—A circumstance or action considered to be unjust; grounds for complaint.

Handicapped—Having a mental or physical impediment or disadvantage that substantially limits an individual's ability to use programs or services.

Health authority—The physician, health administrator, or agency responsible for the provision of health care services at an institution or system of institutions; the responsible physician may be the health authority.

Health care—The sum of all action taken, preventive and therapeutic, to provide for the physical and mental well-being of a population. Includes medical and dental services, mental health services, nursing, personal hygiene, dietary services, and environmental conditions.

Health care personnel—Individuals whose primary duty is to provide health services to inmates in keeping with their respective levels of education, training, and experience.

Health exam—A thorough evaluation of a patient's current physical condition and medical histories conducted by, or under the supervision of, a licensed professional.

Health record—Separate records of medical examinations and diagnoses maintained by the responsible physician. The date and time of all medical examinations and copies of standing or direct medical orders from the physician to facility staff should be transferred to the resident record.

Health screening—A system of structured inquiry and observation designed to prevent newly-arrived inmates who pose a health or safety threat to themselves or others from being admitted to the general population. Screening can be performed by health care personnel or by a health-trained correctional officer at the time of admission.

Health-trained staff person—A person who provides assistance to a physician, nurse, physician's assistant, or other professional medical staff. Duties may include preparing and/or reviewing screening forms for needed followup; preparing inmates and their records for sick call; and assisting in the implementation of medical orders regarding diets, housing, and work assignments.

Hearing—A proceeding to determine a course of action, such as the placement of a juvenile or adult offender, or to determine guilt or innocence in a disciplinary matter. Argument, witnesses, or evidence are heard by a judicial officer or administrative body in making the determination.

Hearing examiner—An individual appointed by the parole authority who conducts hearings for the authority. His or her power of decision making may include, but not be limited to, making parole recommendations to granting, denying, or revoking parole.

Holding facility or lockup—A temporary confinement facility, for which the custodial authority is usually less than forty-eight hours, where arrested persons are held pending release, adjudication, or transfer to another facility.

Glossary

Holidays—All days legally designated as nonworkdays by statute or by the chief governing authority of a jurisdiction.

Housing unit—A group or cluster of single and/or multiple occupancy cells or detention rooms that houses inmates and is immediately adjacent and directly accessible to a day or activity room.

Incident report—A written document reporting a special event such as use of force, use of chemical agents, discharge of firearms, etc. The term is often used interchangeably with the Disciplinary Report.

Independent audit—An audit that is completed independent of influence by the agency or organization being audited.

Independent operator—A person or persons who contracts with a correctional agency or other governmental agency to operate and manage a correctional program or facility.

Indigent—An individual with no funds or source of income.

Industries—An activity existing in a correctional system that uses inmate labor to produce goods and/or services for sale. These goods and/or services are sold at prices calculated to recover all or a substantial portion of costs associated with their production and may include a margin of profit. Sale of the products and/or services is not limited to the institution where the industries activity is located.

Information system—The concepts, personnel, and supporting technology for the collection, organization, and delivery of information for administrative use. There are two such types of information: (1) standard information, consisting of the data required for operational control, such as the daily count, payroll data in a personnel office, probation/parole success rates, referral sources, and caseload levels; and (2) demand information, consisting of information that can be generated when a report is required, such as information on the number of residents in educational and training programs, duration of residency, or the number of residents eligible for discharge during a twelve-month period by offense, sentence, and month of release. (Also referred to as a management information system.)

Informed consent—The agreement by a patient to a treatment, examination, or procedure after the patient receives the material facts regarding the nature, consequences, risks, and alternatives concerning the proposed treatment, examination, or procedure.

Inmate—Any individual, whether in pretrial, unsentenced, or sentenced status, who is confined in a correctional facility.

Inmate compensation—Incentives that are given for services provided. Incentives may be monetary compensation, special housing, extra privileges, good time credits, and other items of value.

Inspection of mail—Examination of incoming and outgoing mail for contraband, cash, checks, and money orders.

Immediate release from locked areas—The capability of immediate staff response that enables the release of all offenders from a locked area to a safe area within four minutes.

Immediate response—The immediate dispatch of assistance to an emergency situation ensuring arrival at the scene within four minutes.

Institution industries manager—The individual designated as responsible for industries operations at a specific institution in the correctional system.

Interstate compact for the supervision of probationers and parolees—An agreement entered into by eligible jurisdictions in the United States and its territories that provides the criteria for these jurisdictions to cooperate in working with probations and releases.

Interstate compact on juveniles—An agreement authorizing the interstate supervision of juvenile delinquents. This can also include the cooperative institutionalization of special types of delinquent juveniles, such as psychotics and defective delinquents.

Judicial review—A proceeding to reexamine the course of action or continued confinement of a juvenile in a secure detention facility. Arguments, witnesses, or evidence are not required as a part of the review. Reviews may be conducted by a judge, judicial officer, or an administrator who has been delegated the authority to release juveniles from secure detention with the approval of the judge.

Juvenile—A person under the age of twenty-one, or as defined in the local jurisdiction as under the age of majority.

Juvenile community residential program—A program housed in a structure without security fences and security hardware or other major restraining construction typically associated with correctional facilities, such as a converted apartment building or private home. They are not constructed as or intended to be detention facilities. Except for daycare programs, they provide twenty-four-hour care, programs, and supervision to juveniles in residence. Their focus is on providing the juvenile with positive adult models and program activities that assist in resolving problems specific to this age group in an environment conducive to positive behavior in the community.

Juvenile detention—Temporary care of juvenile offenders and juveniles alleged to be delinquent who require secure custody in a physically restricting facility.

Juvenile group home—A nonsecure residential program emphasizing family-style living in a homelike atmosphere. Program goals are similar to those for large community residential programs. Although group homes usually house youths who are court-committed, they also house abused or neglected youths who are placed by social agencies. Small group homes serve from four to eight youths; large group homes serve eight to twelve. Their age ranges from ten to seventeen, with the concentration from thirteen to sixteen.

Juvenile intake—The process of determining whether the interests of the public or the juvenile require the filing of a petition with the juvenile court. Generally an intake officer receives, reviews, and processes complaints, recommends detention or release, and provides services for juveniles and their families, including diversion and referral to other community agencies.

Juvenile nonresidential program—A program that provides services to juveniles who live at home and report to the program on a daily basis. Juveniles in these programs require more attention than that provided by probation and aftercare services. Often the program operates its own education program through the local school district. The population of nonresidential programs may be as many as fifty boys and girls ranging in age from ten to eighteen. The population is usually drawn from court commitments but may include juveniles enrolled as a preventive or diversionary measure. The program may operate as part of a residential program, and it may provide space for occasional overnight stays by program participants where circumstances warrant additional assistance.

Juvenile ranch—A nonsecure residential program providing services to youths in a rural setting. Typically, the residents participate in a structured program of education, recreation, and facility maintenance, including responsibility for the physical plant, its equipment, and livestock. Often there are twenty to sixty juveniles in the ranch setting, ranging in age from thirteen to eighteen.

Library service—A service that provides reading materials for convenient use; circulation of reading materials; service to help provide users with library materials, educational and recreational audiovisual materials; or a combination of these services.

Life Safety Code—A manual published and updated by the National Fire Protection Association specifying minimum standards for fire safety necessary in the public interest. Two chapters are devoted to correctional facilities.

Light, natural—Light available from a source within 20 feet of the room/cell with an opening or window that has a view to the outside.

Mail inspection—Examination of incoming and outgoing mail for contraband, cash, checks, and money orders.

Major equipment—All equipment that is securely and permanently fastened to the building or any equipment with current book value of $1,000 or more.

Major infraction—A rule infraction involving a grievous loss and requiring imposition of due process procedures. Major infractions include (1) violations that may result in disciplinary detention or administrative segregation; (2) violations for which punishment may tend to increase an inmate's sentence, such as extending parole eligibility; (3) violations that may result in a forfeiture, such as loss of good-time or work time; and (4) violations that may be referred for criminal prosecution.

Mandatory standards—Standards that have been determined by the American Correctional Association to directly affect the life, health, and safety of offenders and correctional personnel.

Master index file—Used in an institution to keep track of the inmates who are housed in particular housing units.

Measurements, square footage—A measurement of square footage in a room or area as determined by multiplying the length and width of the cell/room and subtracting from that figure the total number of square feet encumbered by bed(s), plumbing fixtures, desk(s), locker(s), and other fixed equipment.

Medical records—Separate records of medical examinations and diagnoses maintained by the responsible physician. The date and time of all medical examinations and copies of standing or direct medical orders from the physician to facility staff should be transferred to the resident record.

Medical restraints—Either chemical restraints, such as sedatives, or physical restraints, such as straitjackets, applied only for medical or psychiatric purposes.

Medical screening—A system of structured observation/initial health assessment to identify newly arrived juvenile or adult offenders who pose a health or safety threat to themselves or others.

Mentally retarded—Describes an individual who functions at a subaverage general intellectual level and is deficient in adaptive behavior.

Minor infraction—A violation of the facility's rules of conduct that does not require due process and can be resolved without the imposition of serious penalties. Minor infractions do not violate any state or federal statutes and may be resolved informally by reporting staff.

Multiple occupancy cell/room—An area designed to house not more than four persons with 35 square feet of unencumbered space for each occupant.

Multiple occupancy housing dormitory—An area, room, or cell housing more than two and less than 50 persons.

Natural light—Light available from an opening or window that has a view to the outside or from a source within 20 feet of the room/cell.

National Fire Protection Association (NFPA)—Publishes the *Life Safety Code*.

National uniform parole reports system—A cooperative effort sponsored by the National Parole Institute that calls for the voluntary cooperation of all federal and state authorities having responsibility for felony offenders in developing some common terms to describe parolees their age, sex, and prior record and some common definitions to describe parole performance. These types of data allow comparisons across states and other jurisdictions.

Noise level, dBA—A system for measuring the relative loudness of sound.

Non-contact visiting—A program that restricts inmates from having physical contact with visitors. Physical barriers usually separate the offender from the visitors with screens and/or glass. Voice communications between the parties are typically accomplished with phones or speakers. Offenders that present a serious escape threat, are a threat to others, or require protection, are often designated for non-contact visits.

Non-mandatory standards—Standards that do not present a direct threat to the life, health, and safety of offenders and staff.

Offender—An individual convicted or adjudicated of a criminal offense.

Official personnel file—A current and accurate record of the employee's job history, including all pertinent information relating to that history.

Operating unit—One distinct operation of the industries activity, which may be operated as a cost center or separate accounting entity. It may take the form of a manufacturing operation (e.g., furniture making, clothing production), an agricultural operation (e.g., dairy or poultry farming, crop or orchard farming, raising beef or pork) or a service activity (e.g., warehouse, keypunch, microfilming, laundering, auto repair, etc.)

Orientation and reception—The reception period includes interviews, testing, and other admissions-related activities, including distribution of information about programs, services, rules, and regulations.

Out-client—An individual who does not live at the facility but who may take advantage of facility services and programs.

Glossary

Parent—The individual with whom a juvenile regularly lives and who is the natural, adoptive, or surrogate parent.

Parent governmental organization—Also referred to as a parent agency, the administrative department or division to whom the agency seeking accreditation reports; the policy-setting body.

Parole authority—The decision-making body that has responsibility to grant, deny, and revoke parole. In some jurisdictions it is called the parole board or the parole commission. The term parole authority includes all of these bodies.

Parole hearing—A procedure conducted by a parole authority member and/or hearing examiner in which all pertinent aspects of an eligible inmate's case are reviewed to make a decision or recommendation that would change the inmate's legal status and/or degree of freedom.

Perimeter security—A system that controls ingress and egress to the interior of a facility or institution. The system may include electronic devices, walls, fences, patrols and/or towers.

Permanent log record—A system of bound records that contain important information. Typically, permanent logs regard emergency situations and/or unusual incidents. Length of retention is dependent upon the governing agency's policy or legislation.

Permanent status—A personnel status that provides due process protection prior to dismissal.

Personal property—Property that legally belongs to the inmate/juvenile.

Petition—An application for a court order or other judicial action. For example, a delinquency petition is an application for the court to act in the matter of a juvenile apprehended for a delinquent act.

Physical examination—A thorough evaluation of a patient's current physical condition and medical history conducted by or under the supervision of a licensed professional.

Plan of action—Detailed statement of actions which will be taken by the agency to achieve compliance with a standard. The plan designates staff responsibilities and timetables for completing each task.

Placing authority—The agency or body with the authority to order a juvenile into a specific dispositional placement. This may be the juvenile court, the probation department, or another duly constituted and authorized placement agency.

Policy—A course of action adopted by and pursued by an agency that guides and determines present and future decisions and actions. Policies indicate the general course or direction of an organization within which the activities of the personnel must operate.

Population center—A geographical area containing at least 10,000 people, along with public safety services, professional services, employment and educational opportunities, and cultural/recreational opportunities.

Preliminary hearing—A hearing to determine probable cause for revoking parole pending a revocation hearing. This term is used interchangeably with Probable cause hearing.

Pretrial release—A procedure whereby an accused individual who had been taken into custody is allowed to be released before and during his or her trial.

Preventive maintenance—A system designed to enhance the longevity and/or usefulness of buildings and equipment in accordance with a planned schedule.

Probable cause hearing—See *Preliminary hearing*.

Probation—A court-ordered disposition alternative through which a convicted adult offender or an adjudicated delinquent is placed under the control, supervision, and care of a probation field staff member.

Probationary period—A period of time designated to evaluate and test an employee to ascertain fitness for the job. This period lasts at least six months but no longer than one year.

Procedure—The detailed and sequential actions that must be executed to ensure that a policy is implemented. It is the method of performing an operation or a manner of proceeding on a course of action. It differs from a policy in that it directs action required to perform a specific task within the guidelines of the policy.

Professional association—A collective body of individuals engaged in a particular profession or vocation. The American Correctional Association, the American Medical Association, and the National Association of

Clinical Psychologists are examples of professional associations, of which there are hundreds in the United States.

Professional staff—Social workers, probation officers, and other staff assigned to juvenile and adult offender cases. These individuals generally possess bachelor's degrees and advanced training in the social or behavioral sciences.

Program—The plan or system through which a correctional agency works to meet its goals; often this program requires a distinct physical setting, such as a correctional institution, community residential facility, group home, or foster home.

Program director—The individual directly in charge of the program, who may also be called the administrator, superintendent, or houseparent.

Protective custody—A status that describes inmates requesting or requiring protection from others.

Private agency—The unit of governing authority that has direct responsibility for the operation of a corrections program.

Public agency—The governing authority that has direct responsibility for the operation of a corrections program.

Rated capacity—The original architectural design capacity plus or minus capacity changes resulting from building additions, reductions, or revisions.

Records (juvenile and adult offenders)—Information concerning the individual's delinquent or criminal, personal, and medical history and behavior and activities while in custody, including but not limited to commitment papers, court orders, detainers, personal property receipts, visitors lists, photographs, fingerprints, type of custody, disciplinary infractions and actions taken, grievance reports, work assignments, program participation, and miscellaneous correspondence.

Referral—The process by which a juvenile or adult offender is introduced to an agency or service that can provide the assistance needed.

Release on bail—The release by a judicial officer of an accused individual who has been taken into custody. The accused promises to appear in court as required for criminal proceedings.

Releasing authority—The decision-making body and/or individual that has the responsibility to grant, deny, and revoke release from a juvenile institution or program of supervision. In some jurisdictions it is called the parole board or the parole commission. (See *Aftercare*.)

Religious faith judicatory—Practices that are enforced by a religious faith that prescribes access to religious publications, religious symbols, worship/religious services, religious study classes, and adherence to dietary requirements.

Renovation—A significant structural or design change in the physical plant of a facility.

Research—A systematic search for facts or scientific investigation.

Responsible physician—An individual licensed to practice medicine and provide health services to the inmate population of the facility and/or the physician at an institution with final responsibility for decisions related to medical judgments.

Restraints—Devices used to restrict physical activity. Handcuffs, leg irons, and straight jackets are typically classified as restraints.

Revocation hearing—A hearing before the parole authority at which it is determined whether revocation of parole should be made final.

Rulebook, inmate—A collection of the facility's rules of conduct and sanctions for violations, defined in writing.

Safety equipment—Primarily firefighting equipment, e.g., chemical extinguishers, hoses, nozzles, water supplies, alarm systems, sprinkler systems, portable breathing devices, gas masks, fans, first aid kits, stretchers, and emergency alarms.

Glossary

Safety vestibule—In a correctional facility, a grill cage that divides the inmate areas from the remainder of the institution. It must have two doors or gates, only one of which opens at a time, to permit entry to or exit from inmate areas in a safe and controlled manner.

Sally port—An enclosure situated in the perimeter wall or fence of a correctional facility containing gates or doors at both ends, only one of which opens at a time, ensuring there will be no breach in the perimeter security of the institution. The sally port may handle either pedestrian or vehicular traffic.

Secure institution—Any facility that is designed and operated to ensure that all entrances and exits are under the exclusive control of the facility's staff, thereby not allowing an inmate/resident to leave the facility unsupervised or without permission.

Security or custody—The degree of restriction of inmate movement within a detention/correctional facility, usually divided into maximum, medium, and minimum risk levels.

Security devices—Locks, gates, doors, bars, fences, screens, ceilings, floors, walls, and barriers used to confine and control detained individuals. Also included are electronic monitoring equipment, security alarm systems, security light units, auxiliary power supplies, and other equipment used to maintain facility security.

Security perimeter—The outer portions of a facility that provide for secure confinement of facility inmates/residents. The design of the perimeter may vary depending on the security classification of the facility.

Segregation—The confinement of an inmate to an individual cell that is separated from the general population. There are three forms of segregation: administrative segregation, disciplinary detention, and protective custody.

Segregation unit—A housing section that separates inmates who threaten the security or orderly management of the institution from the general population.

Self-insurance coverage—A statewide system designed to insure the payment of all legal claims for injury or damage incurred as a result of the actions of state officials, employees, or agents. In public agencies, the self-insurance program is usually authorized by the legislature. A "memorandum of insurance" or similar document is required that acts as a policy, setting the limits of liability for various categories of risk, including deductible limits. Approval of the policy by a cabinet-level official is also required.

Serious incident—A situation in which injury serious enough to warrant medical attention occurs involving a resident, employee, or visitor on the grounds of the institution. Also, a situation containing an imminent threat to the security of the institution and/or to the safety of residents, employees, or visitors on the grounds of the institution.

Severe mental disturbance—A condition in which an individual is a danger to self or others or is incapable of attending to basic physiological needs.

Shelter facility—Any nonsecure public or private facility designated to provide either temporary placement for alleged or adjudicated status offenders prior to the issuance of a disposition order or longer-term care under a juvenile court disposition order.

Sheriff—The elected or appointed chief executive officer of a county law enforcement agency. Sheriffs can serve several functions, including responsibility for law enforcement in unincorporated areas, operation of the county jail, and assignment as officers of the court.

Single cell/room—An area designed to house one person with at least 35 square feet of unencumbered space.

Special management inmate—An individual who presents a serious threat to the safety and security of the facility, staff, general inmate population, or himself/herself.

Special needs inmate—An inmate whose mental and/or physical condition requires special handling and treatment by staff. Special needs inmates include, but are not limited to, drug or alcohol addicts or abusers, the emotionally disturbed, mentally retarded, suspected mentally ill, physically handicapped, chronically ill, and the disabled or infirm.

Status offender—A youth who has been charged with or adjudicated for conduct that under the law of the jurisdiction in which the offense was committed would not be a crime if committed by an adult. (See *Delinquent youth*.)

Strip search—An examination of an inmate/resident's naked body for weapons, contraband, and physical abnormalities. This also includes a thorough search of all of the individual's clothing while it is not being worn.

Summer and winter comfort zones—Suggested temperature ranges for indoor living and work areas during the summer months are 66 to 86 degrees Fahrenheit and 61 to 73 degrees Fahrenheit in the winter months.

Temporary release—A period of time during which an offender is allowed to leave the program or institution and go into the community unsupervised for various purposes consistent with public interest.

Training—An organized, planned, and evaluated activity designed to achieve specific learning objectives and enhance the job performance of personnel. Training may occur on-site, at an academy or training center, an institution of higher learning, professional meetings, or through supervised on-the-job training. It includes an agenda and is conducted by an instructor, manager, or official. Meetings of professional associations are considered training. Whether it occurs on-site, at an academy or training center, through contract services, or at professional meetings, the activity must be part of an overall training program.

Training plan—A set of long- or short-range training activities that equip staff with the knowledge, skills, and attitudes they need to accomplish the goals of the agency.

Training school—Also known as a youth development center, youth village, youth correction center, youth treatment center, youth service center, or school or home for boys and girls. The typical training school may provide supervision, programs, and residential services for more than 100 residents; however, programs of this size are not encouraged. (Standards for new facilities require that each new training school have no more than 100 beds and be limited to two stories in height.) These facilities are designed and operated to be secure institutions.

Youth development centers, youth treatment centers, secure training schools, and other facilities in this category may serve relatively smaller populations ranging from forty to 100 juveniles. The age range served is generally from thirteen to eighteen, although in many jurisdictions residents may be as young as ten or as old as twenty. Older residents are usually juveniles who have been returned to the facility as parole violators.

Treatment plan—A series of written statements that specify the particular course of therapy and the roles of medical and nonmedical personnel in carrying it out. A treatment plan is individualized, based on assessment of the individual patient's needs, and includes a statement of the short- and long-term goals and the methods by which the goals will be pursued. When clinically indicated, the treatment plan provides inmates with access to a range of supportive and rehabilitative services, e.g., individual or group counseling and/or self-help groups that the physician deems appropriate.

Unencumbered cell space—A measurement of square footage in a room or area obtained by multiplying the length and width of the cell/room and subtracting from that figure the total number of square feet encumbered by bed(s), plumbing fixtures, desk(s), locker(s), and other fixed equipment.

Unit, correctional housing—A group or cluster of single and/or multiple occupancy cells or detention rooms within a facility that houses inmates and is immediately adjacent and directly accessible to a day or activity room.

Unit management—A management system that subdivides an institution into units. The unit management system has several basic requirements:

1. Each unit holds a relatively small number of inmates. Ideally, there should be less than 150 but not more than 500 inmates.
2. Inmates are housed in the same unit for a major portion of their confinement.
3. Inmates that are assigned to the unit work in a close relationship with a multidisciplinary team of staff who are regularly assigned to the unit and whose offices are located within the unit.
4. Staff members have decision-making authority for the institutional programming and living conditions for the inmates assigned to the unit within broad rules, policies, and guidelines established by the agency and/or the facility administrator.
5. Inmate assignments to a unit are based on the inmate's need for control, security, and programs offered.

Unit management increases contact between staff and inmates, fosters increased interpersonal relationships, and leads to more knowledgeable decision making as a direct result of staff dealing with a smaller, more

Glossary

permanent group. At the same time, the facility benefits from the economies inherent in centralized service facilities, such as utilities, food service, health care, educational systems, vocational programs, and recreational facilities.

Urine surveillance program—A program whereby urine samples are collected on an irregular basis from offenders suspected of having a history of drug use to determine current or recent use.

Visits, extended—Visits between inmates and their families, either on institutional grounds or at the home.

Volunteer, citizen—An individual who donates time and/or effort to enhance the activities and programs of the agency. They are selected on the basis of their skills and personal qualities to provide services in a variety of activities such as recreation, counseling, education, and religion.

Waiver—A decision made by the accreditation panel not to require an agency to submit a plan-of-action for a standard that is in noncompliance. Waivers are typically granted when it is determined that the totality of conditions do not present an imminent threat to the life and safety of occupants. Waivers may also be granted when it is apparent that a plan-of-action is impossible and if the condition does not pose imminent threat.

Warden/Superintendent—The individual in charge of the institution; the chief executive or administrative officer. This position is sometimes referred to by other titles, but warden and superintendent are the most commonly used terms.

Work release—An arrangement sanctioned by law that enables an inmate/resident to be released into the community to maintain approved employment and/or other approved activity.

Workmen's compensation—A statewide system of benefits for employees who are disabled by job-related injury.

Work stoppage—A planned or spontaneous discontinuation of work. The stoppage may involve employees or inmates acting separately, or in concert, by refusing to participate in institutional activities.

ACCREDITATION STAFF
1976 - 1990

Allison, Jeff
Ashburn, Kevin
Barry, Gina
Bergsmann, Ilene
Boker, Richard
Boyd, Lois
Burkhardt, Suzanne
Butler, Deborah
Callies, Joy
Calpin, Laura
Davis, Beverly B.
Dezell, Thomas
Dixon, Alexandreena D.
Dunn, Susan Ainsle
Fetter, Jeroldine
Fosen, Robert H., Ph.D.
Gentilucci, Tracy
Glidden, Brenda
Gooding, Howard M.
Green, Myrna
Greene, John J. III
Greene, Peggy
Heflin, Lloyd W.
Howard, Roberta L.
Jenness, Susan
Johnson, Juanita
Johnson, Sharon
Kennedy, Karen
Keesling, Carol
Kushner, Karen

Levinson, Robert B., Ph.D.
Lewis-Lloyd, Cynthia
Medley, Grace
Miller, Dodie
Miller, Susan S.
Neagle, Ken
O'Shaughnessy, Jane A.
Pacanowski, Christine
Powers, Bettie
Price, Shelley J.
Pritchard, Lynn
Pusateri, Linde
Rauch, W. Hardy
Reimer, Ernest G., M.S.W.
Reusing, Charles R.
Ruppe, Gail
Sechrest, Dale
Shaw, Debbie
Shaw, Delores
Slattery, Kerrie
Smalley, Karen
Swahl, Carol
Tuller, Sue
Verdeyen, Robert
Vogel, Ruth
Washington, Jeffrey
West, Jean
White, Stephanie
Winkler, Sharon J.

MEMBERS OF THE STANDARDS COMMITTEE
1976 - 1990

Albrecht, Thomas, DC, 1988 - 1990
Allen, Frederick R., NY, 1982 - 1986, 1988 - 1990
Angelone, Ron, NV, 1986 - 1988
Atchison, Jim, KY, 1976 - 1978
Bailey, Paul E., NV, 1980 - 1982
Black, James, CO, 1988 - 1990
Blake, Gary R., GA, 1986 - 1988
Belleque, Lester E., OR, 1982 - 1986
Bertrand, Roma, CN, 1984 - 1986
Braithwaite, John W., CN, 1976 - 1980
Breed, Allen F., DC, 1976 - 1982
Brown, Robert, Jr., MI, 1988 - 1990
Brutsche, Robert L., M.D., VA, 1988 - 1990
Campbell, Nancy M., WA, 1986 - 1988
Carlson, Norman A., DC, 1976 - 1978
Chamberlain, Norman F., WA, 1980 - 1982
Clute, Penelope D., NY, 1988 - 1990
Coleman, Ray, WA, 1986 - 1988
Collins, William C., WA, 1984 - 1986
Coughlin, Thomas A., NY, 1988 - 1990
Crist, Roger W., CO, 1982 - 1984
Crawford, Jacqueline, AZ, 1976 - 1990
Davis, Pamela Jo, FL, 1986 - 1990
Decell, Grady A., SC, 1979 - 1982
Dismukes, Hugh C., TX, 1980 - 1982
Dorsey, Helen Brown, WA, 1982 - 1984
Dorsey, Neil, MD, 1982 - 1984
Enomoto, J. J., CA, 1979 - 1980
Estelle, W. J., Jr.,TX, 1976 - 1980
Evans, David C., GA, 1988 - 1990
Farkas, Gerald M., DC, 1978 - 1986
Farrier, Harold A., IA, 1986 - 1990
Gagnon, John R., WI, 1976 - 1980
Gamby, Jacqueline Jones, CO, 1980 - 1986
Gaudio, Anthony C., VA, 1976 - 1978
Giesen, Linda, IL, 1982 - 1984
Gispert, Ana, FL, 1982 - 1984
Goodall, Paula, OK, 1982 - 1984
Guillen, Rudy F., VA, 1976 - 1982
Hahn, Paul H., OH, 1984 - 1986
Hatrak, Robert, NV, 1984 - 1986
Hill, Gary, NE, 1976 - 1978 - 1980
Holden, Tamara, UT, 1986 - 1988
Housewright, Vernon G., IL, 1976 -1982, 1984 - 1986
Humphrey-Barnett, Susan, AK, 1988 - 1990

Irving, James R., IL, 1988 - 1990
Jackson, Ronald G., TX, 1978 - 1980
Johnson, Perry M., MI, 1984 - 1990
Jordan, James M., IL, 1986 - 1988
Kehoe, Charles J., MI, 1978 - 1982
Kelley, Marton, OH, 1976 - 1978
Lejins, Peter P., MD, 1976 - 1978
Livingston, Shirley H., FL, 1976 - 1979
Maynard, Gary D., OK, 1989 - 1990
McCartt, John M., OH, 1976 - 1978
McCotter, O. L., TX, 1984 - 1986
McMahon, John F., NY, 1976 - 1978
Milliken, William V., UT, 1982 - 1984
Mitchell, Anabel P., FL, 1984 - 1986
Morton, Joann B., SC, 1976 - 1980
Myers, Victoria C., MO, 1980 - 1982
Nelson, Ray, CO, 1984 - 1986
Pappert, Ruth M., IN, 1980 - 1982
Patterson, Wayne K., CO, 1976 - 1978
Petrovsky, Joseph, MO, 1982 - 1984
Phyfer, George M., AL, 1976 - 1978
Pointer, W. Donald, MD, 1978 - 1980
Pugh, Julian U., VA, 1978 - 1980
Quinlan, J. Michael, DC, 1986 - 1990
Rapp, Marcella, CO, 1984 - 1986
Rees, John D., NM, 1988 - 1990
Robinson, Carl, CT, 1982 - 1984
Robinson, William B., PA, 1980 - 1984
Robuck, Lucille, KY, 1976 - 1978
Rosser, Paul, GA, 1984 - 1986
Rossi, Linda D'Amario, RI, 1980 - 1982
Shirley, Sue, TX, 1980 - 1982
Shope, John T., NC, 1976 - 1978
Schmidt, Robert, DC, 1986 - 1988
Sipos, Chiquita, CA, 1984 - 1986
Sublett, Samuel, Jr., IL, 1976 - 1986
Swanson, Virginia, WA, 1988 - 1990
Vassar, B. Norris, VA, 1986 - 1988
Ward, Frederick J., NJ, 1976 - 1978
Weber, J. Robert, NC, 1982 - 1984
Weldon, Paul I., SC, 1978 - 1980
White, William S., IL, 1986 - 1988
Wilson, George W., OH, 1988 - 1990
Wirkler, Norman E., CO, 1988 - 1990
Wrenshall, Allan F., CN, 1982 - 1984
Young, Marjorie H., GA, 1986 - 1988

MEMBERS OF THE
COMMISSION ON ACCREDITATION FOR CORRECTIONS
1974 - 1990

Ackermann, John, NY, 1976 - 1977
Black, James, CO, 1986 - 1988*
Blake, Gary, MD, 1979 - 1984
Braithwaite, John, CN, 1980 - 1986
Brutsche, Robert L., M.D., VA, 1986 - 1992
Charters, Paul, FL, 1979 - 1984
Clute, Penelope D., NY, 1984 - 1990
Coate, Alfred B., MT, 1975 - 1980
Cocoros, John, TX, 1988 - 1994
Coleman, Raymond J., WA, 1984 - 1990
Crawford, Jacqueline, AZ, 1986 - 1992
Dietz, Christopher D., NJ, 1980 - 1986
Dunbar, Walter, NY, 1974 - 1975
Elias, Al, NJ, 1979 - 1980
Elrod, Richard J., IL, 1984 - 1986
Enomoto, J. J., CA, 1980 - 1986
Evans, David C., GA, 1988 - 1994
Fant, Fred D., NJ, 1974 - 1978
Farkas, Gerald M., PA, 1974 - 1978
Fryer, Gordon L., IL, 1974 - 1978
George, B. James, Jr., NY, 1979 - 1984
Gladstone, William E., FL, 1981 - 1986
Goodrich, Edna L., WA, 1978 - 1982
Green, Leslie R., MN, 1979 - 1984
Hammergren, Donald R., MN, 1975 - 1979
Hays, Bonnie L., OR, 1987 - 1992
Heard, John, TX, 1974 - 1978
Heyne, Robert P., IN, 1974 - 1977
Hopkins, Wayne, DC, 1974 - 1977
Huggins, M. Wayne, VA, 1983 - 1988*
Irving, James R., IL, 1981 - 1986
Jefferson, Ralph A., WI, 1978 - 1983
Johnson, Perry M., MI, 1986 - 1992
Jordan, James M., IL, 1984 - 1990
Kehoe, Charles J., MD, 1983 - 1988
Lucas, William, MI, 1978 - 1983

Maciekowich, Z. C., AZ, 1974 - 1975
Mangogna, Thomas J., MO, 1974 - 1979
Martinez, Orlando L., CO, 1986 - 1992
McGough, John, WA, 1979 - 1984
Minor, John, MI, 1988 - 1994
Moeller, H. G., NC, 1974 - 1980
Moore, Edgar C. (Ted), SC, 1982 - 1988*
Morrissey, Thomas H., NC, 1979 - 1980
Myers, Victoria C., MO, 1982 - 1988*
Newberger, Jay M., SD, 1984 - 1990
Nichols, R. Raymond, ME, 1974 - 1976
Nuernberger, W. W., NE, 1974 - 1979
Omodt, Don, MN, 1979 - 1980
Orlando, Frank A., FL, 1986 - 1992
Patterson, Wayne K., CO, 1978 - 1983
Phyfer, George M., AL, 1986 - 1992
Pointer, W. Donald, MD, 1974 - 1977
Quinn, Luke, MI, 1988 - 1994
Rapp, Marcella C., CO, 1977 - 1982
Reed, Amos E., NC, 1976 - 1981
Riedman, Irvin M., ND, 1975 - 1980
Rodriguez, Felix, NM, 1979 - 1980
Rossi, Linda D'Amario, RI, 1981 - 1986
Rowan, Joseph R., IL, 1974 - 1980
Shirley, Sue, TX, 1981 - 1986
Skoler, Daniel, DC, 1974 - 1979
Swanson, Virginia, WA, 1984 - 1990
Tremont, J. Steven, LA, 1977 - 1982
Van DeKamp, John, CA, 1974 - 1976
Watson, Robert J., OR, 1977 - 1982
Weber, J. Robert, KY, 1974 - 1981
Wheeler, Martha E., MI, 1974 - 1977
White, William S., IL, 1983 - 1988
Wilson, George W., KY, 1982 - 1988*
Wirkler, Norman E., CO, 1984 - 1990
Young, Marjorie H., GA, 1986 - 1992

*Based on an extension of original term in order to correspond with ACA election year

THE AMERICAN CORRECTIONAL ASSOCIATION
MEMBERS OF THE BOARD OF GOVERNORS
DURING THE STANDARDS AND ACCREDITATION ERA
1974 - 1990

Adamek, F. Jerald, CO, 1976 - 1978
Agee, Vicki L., OH, 1986 - 1988
Andersen, Carolyn, UT, 1984 - 1986
Anderson, Charles, ID, 1974 - 1975
Avery, Dennis, MN, 1988 - 1990
Avery, Michael T., TX, 1975 - 1976
Barker, Marjorie H., IN, 1976 - 1980
Barrington, R. W., CN, 1976 - 1978
Bergen, Donna R., MO, 1986 - 1988
Belleque, Les, OR, 1980 - 1984
Beto, George, TX, 1974 - 1976
Bills, John D., ID, 1974 - 1976
Bishop, Frank B. III, VA, 1980 - 1984
Black, James T., DC, 1980 - 1982
Black, Lee Roy, MO, 1984 - 1988
Black, Raymond M., CA, 1975 - 1976
Blanchard, Don E., UT, 1986 - 1988
Blanton, Jack V., FL, 1974 - 1976
Bowman, Jon G., WA, 1978 - 1990
Boyle, Edward C., CA, 1974 - 1976
Brahe, Champ K., FL, 1978 - 1990
Braithwaite, John W., CN, 1974 - 1975
Breed, Allen F., CA, 1974 - 1976,
 1984 - 1988
Breslin, Maurice, OH, 1974 - 1975
Brewer, Ernesteen, TN, 1974 - 1975
Brown, Robert, Jr., MI, 1988 - 1990
Bruce, Ronald D., ID, 1976 - 1978
Bryant, Robert C., KY, 1975 - 1976
Byrd, John W., TX, 1986 - 1988
Cain, Robert D., Jr., AZ, 1976 - 1990
Callanan, Thomas J., CA, 1984 - 1986
Campbell, John D., NC, 1974 - 1978
Carson, Ronald, WA, 1976 - 1978
Carlson, Norman A., DC, 1974 - 1982
Casas, Anthony, CA, 1982 - 1984
Case, John, PA, 1974 - 1975
Cass, E. R., NY, 1974 - 1976
Charters, Paul J., FL, 1975 - 1980
Ciuros, William, Jr., NY, 1984 - 1988
Cocoros, John A., TX, 1982 - 1984
Coffey, Betsy, KY, 1982 - 1986
Colvin, Kaye H., CO, 1974 - 1978
Cooper, Bennett J., OH, 1975 - 1976,
 1982 - 1988
Corbett, Gary, CO, 1976 - 1978
Corrothers, Helen G., DC, 1980 - 1990
Crawford, Fred L., FL, 1988 - 1990

Crawford, Jacqueline, AZ, 1975 - 1976,
 1980-1982
Culpepper, Judy, TX, 1988 - 1990
Cunningham, Chester R., CN, 1982 - 1986
Cunningham, Su, TX, 1982 - 1990
Davis, Mary C., NY, 1976 - 1978
Davis, Pamela Jo, FL, 1988 - 1990
Davis, Rendell A., PA, 1984 - 1986
Decell, Grady A., SC, 1978 - 1980
DeHart, Doris, VA, 1980 - 1982
Denton, George, OH, 1974 - 1975
Dunlap, Earl L., KY, 1986 - 1988
Dye, Larry L., NY, 1988 - 1990
Eastland, Charles, KY, 1978 - 1980
Emmelhainz, Edgar, Jr., FL, 1976 - 1978
Erickson, Don R., ID, 1974 - 1978
Estelle, W. J., Jr., TX, 1975 - 1980
Evan, Mary Ann, OR, 1976 - 1978
Evans, Walter, OR, 1975 - 1976
Farkas, Gerald M., MD, 1980 - 1982
Ferris, Jane, MD, 1976 - 1978
Freeman, Robert A., WA, 1974 - 1978
Gable, Katherine, MA, 1976 - 1978
Gagnon, John R., WI, 1978 - 1980
Gaudio, Anthony, VA, 1976 - 1978
Gispert, Ana I., FL, 1984 - 1990
Gondles, James A., Jr., VA, 1986 - 1990
Gubbins, Edmund, CT, 1974 - 1975
Guillen, Rudy, VA, 1975 - 1976
Hahn, Paul H., OH, 1976 - 1978, 1982 - 1984
Hall, Frank A., MD, 1982 - 1984
Hammergren, Donald R., MN, 1974 - 1975,
 1982 - 1984
Hardesty, George A., KY, 1976 - 1978,
 1980 -1982
Hatrak, Robert S., NV, 1982 - 1984
Hill, Gary, NE, 1974 - 1976, 1982 - 1984
Hill, Jerry D., CA, 1986 - 1988
Hopkins, Arnold J., MD, 1984 - 1986
Howard, Ray E., FL, 1975 - 1976
Housewright, Vernon G., IL, 1975 - 1980
Hunter, Susan M., DC, 1984 - 1986
Hubanks, Allan C., FL, 1974 - 1975
Hughes, Gail, MO, 1974 - 1975
Huskey, Bobbie L., IL, 1984 - 1986,
 1988 - 1990
Hutto, T. Don, TN, 1982 - 1988
Jackson, Ronald G., TX, 1978 - 1980

Johnson, Perry M., MI, 1980 - 1984
Johnson, Terry L., OR, 1974 - 1975
Kehoe, Charles J., MI, 1974 - 1975,
   1978 - 1982
Kehoe, John, CA, 1974 - 1975
Keller, Oliver J., FL, 1974 - 1978
Killinger, George G., TX, 1980 - 1982
Koenning, Keith A., CO, 1975 - 1978
Kuharich, Anthony S., IL, 1974 - 1978
Leeke, William D., SC, 1974 - 1980
Lejins, Peter P., MD, 1974 - 1976
Lightsey, Michael, TX, 1976 - 1978
Lindsey, John W., TX, 1974 - 1976
Livingston, Shirley H., FL, 1974 - 1976
Maciekowich, Z. D., AZ, 1974 - 1975
Mahoney, Michael J., IL, 1988 - 1990
Maloney, Francis H., CT, 1975 - 1976
Mangogna, Thomas J., MO, 1974 - 1976
Marshall, Ralph O., ID, 1976 - 1978
McCartt, John M., OH, 1974 - 1980
McGee, Thomas, CA, 1974 - 1975
McMahon, John F., NY, 1976 - 1978
Mercantino, Anthony, NJ, 1974 - 1975
Milliken, William V., FL, 1984 - 1986,
   1988 - 1990
Moeller, H. G., NC, 1974 - 1976, 1980 - 1986
Moll, Robert A., KY, 1975 - 1976
Morton, Joann B., SC, 1975 - 1978,
   1980 - 1982
Murray, Lane, TX, 1975 - 1980
Myers, Victoria, MO, 1982 - 1984
Nardini, William, IN, 1974 - 1976
Nelson, JoAnn Longo, WA, 1986 - 1990
Norman, George W., Jr., MO, 1976 - 1978
Northen, Thomas J. III, VA, 1980 - 1982
Olsen, Raymond S., DC, 1974 - 1976
O'Sullivan, James P., CN, 1982 - 1984,
   1986 - 1988
Page, Donald M., CN, 1988 - 1990
Pappert, Ruth M., IN, 1978 - 1980
Patterson, Wayne K., CO, 1976 - 1978
Pease, Robert C., NE, 1975 - 1976
Penny, Lawrence D., KS, 1974 - 1978
Peters, Howard A. III, IL, 1984 - 1986
Pinckney, Vergil M., MI, 1984 - 1988
Pogue, Edwin T., NV, 1976 - 1978
Pointer, W. Donald, MD, 1975 - 1978
Poole, Harry W., FL, 1984 - 1986
Pugh, Julian U., VA, 1978 - 1980

Quinlan, J. Michael, DC, 1988 - 1990
Rapp, Marcella, CO, 1974 - 1984
Reed, Amos, WA, 1978 - 1984
Reina, Charles F., CT, 1984 - 1986
Rhay, B. J., WA, 1974 - 1975
Riley, J. Bryan, MA, 1980 - 1984,
   1988 - 1990
Robinson, Carl, CT, 1980 - 1982
Rodriquez, Felix, NM, 1974 - 1980
Rossi, Linda D'Amario, MD, 1986 - 1990
Roush, David W., MI, 1988 - 1990
Ruth, Harry I., MO, 1976 - 1978
Schoenbacher, R. O. D., TX, 1975 - 1978
Seidler, Carl A., MD, 1975 - 1976
Sellers, Bertis H., NC, 1978 - 1980
Sheridan, Eugene T., MO, 1976 - 1978
Shirley, Sue, TX, 1980 - 1982
Sipos, Chiquita A., CA, 1984 - 1986,
   1988 - 1990
Smith, L. D., ID, 1974 - 1980
Smith, Rex, MD, 1980 - 1982
Stepanik, Ronald, FL, 1988 - 1990
Stith, Ann Carter, MO, 1974 - 1975
Strickland, Katherine G., AZ, 1974 - 1976
Sublett, Samuel, Jr., IL, 1975 - 1978,
   1986 - 1990
Swanson, Virginia, WA, 1982 - 1984
Taylor, Donald W., TX, 1986 - 1988
Tiku, Jatindar M., DE, 1975 - 1976
Todman, Lionel A., VA, 1975 - 1976
Torres, Ruben M., TX, 1980 - 1984
Tracy, Chris, TX, 1980 - 1982
Travisono, Anthony P., MD, 1974 - 1990
Troje, Bernard M., MN, 1975 - 1976
Umina, Anthony, NY, 1986 - 1988
Vermillion, W. R., MO, 1976 - 1978
Walker, Charles W., OH, 1974 - 1976
Walsh, James F., MO, 1975 - 1978
Watson, Robert J., DE, 1986 - 1990
Weis, Raymond J., KY, 1975 - 1978
Weldon, Paul I., SC, 1978 - 1980
Wells, J. D., TX, 1974 - 1975
West, Pearl, CA, 1980 - 1982
Whitson, Charles M., OH, 1976 - 1978
Winans, Harvey D., WI, 1984 - 1986
Wolford, Bruce I., KY, 1986 - 1990
Wright, Roberts J., ME, 1974 - 1975
Young, Jack G., MN, 1975 - 1976

Index

ACADEMIC PROGRAMS (See EDUCATION: Academic/vocational programs)
ADMINISTRATION
    Administrative manual 1A-02
    Administrative officer (See also WARDEN/ SUPERINTENDENT) 1A-06, 07
    Communication channels 1A-16
    Community involvement (See also COMMUNITY RELATIONS) 1A-05
    Delegation of authority 1A-16
    Employee/management relations 1C-01
    Goals
        long-range 1B-03
        mission 1A-02
        short-range 1A-03
    Inmate programs (See PROGRAMS)
    Inspection systems (See also INSPECTIONS) 1A-17
    Legal assistance 1A-20
    Information dissemination (See INFORMATION DISSEMINATION)
    Organizational chart 1A-14
    Public information program (See also INFORMATION DISSEMINATION) 1F-03
    Policy and procedure 1A-14; 1G-07
        dissemination 1A-15
        formulation 1A-04, 05, 15; 1G-09
        manual 1A-13, 14; 1C-01; 3A-01
        review (See also ANNUAL REVIEW: Policies and procedures) 4E-04
    Political involvement 1A-21; 1C-23
    Quarterly reports (See also REPORTS) 1A-18
    Staff
        meetings 1A-16
        participation 1A-04; 1B-03
    Statutory authority 1A-01, 08; 3A-31
    Unit management 1A-06, 14
    Vehicles 1B-15; 3A-23, 24
    Work stoppage 3B-13
ADMINISTRATIVE SEGREGATION (See SEGREGATION)
ADMISSION PROCEDURES 4A-01
    Admission report 4A-01, 04
    Classification (See also CLASSIFICATION) 4B-01
    Housing assignment 4E-37, 38
    Inmate clothing 4D-08
    Intake 1F-07
    Medical screening/appraisal 4E-19, 20, 21, 22
    Orientation 4A-01, 02, 03; 4E-06
        materials 4A-01; 3C-03
    Personal property (See also INMATE PERSONAL PROPERTY) 4A-04
    Reception 4A-01
    Telephone Calls 5D-09
AFFIRMATIVE ACTION (See EQUAL EMPLOYMENT OPPORTUNITIES)
ANNUAL REVIEW
    Inmate rules 3C-01
    Mission statement 1A-02
    Organizational chart 1A-11
    Performance review 1C-16
    Plans 1C-07; 1D-01; 3B-11, 14; 4B-01
    Policies and procedures 1A-12, 13, 14; 1C-02; 2F-02; 3B-02, 15; 3C-02; 4B-01; 4E-04; 5D-01
    Post orders 3A-05
BUDGET (See FISCAL MANAGEMENT)
CASE RECORDS
    Confidentiality 1E-01; 1G-07; 4E-47
    Content 1E-01, 03, 06
        admission report 4A-01
        disciplinary report 3C-20
        good time record 1E-03
        personal property receipt 4A-04
    Disclosure 1E-01
    Inmate access 1E-04
    Management 1E-01, 06
    Master file 1F-04; 3D-15
    Policy and procedure 1E-01
    Release-of-information 1E-05
    Transfers 1E-02; 4E-48
CHIEF EXECUTIVE OFFICER (See WARDEN/SUPERINTENDENT)
CITIZEN INVOLVEMENT(See also VOLUNTEERS) 1A-05; 5A-11
    Programs 1G-01, 02
CLASSIFICATION
    Appeals 4B-02
    Classification plan 4B-01, 02
    Custody level 3D-05, 06; 4B-04
    Health care needs 3D-05
    Hearings 3D-05
    Procedures 4B-01, 02
    Program status review 1A-01; 3D-05, 06; 4B-02
    Special needs inmates (See also SPECIAL NEEDS INMATES) 4B-03
        juveniles 4B-04
COEDUCATIONAL FACILITIES 3E-05
COMMUNITY RELATIONS
    Citizen involvement program 1G-01, 02
    Community involvement 1A-05; 5A-11
    Community resources (See COMMUNITY RESOURCES)

Index

Information dissemination (See also INFORMATION DISSEMINATION) 1A-19; 1F-03
Volunteers (See VOLUNTEERS)

COMMUNITY RESOURCES
　Education programs 5B-02
　Employee training program 1D-05
　Purchasing 1B-13
　Recreation 5C-01
　Religious services 5F-03, 05
　Social services 4F-02
　Work programs 5A-11

CONFIDENTIALITY
　Case records 1E-05
　　policy and procedure 1E-01
　Health records 4E-47
　Information systems 1F-02, 09
　Inmate rights 1C-24; 1E-05; 1G-07; 3E-02
　Media 1A-19
　Personnel 1C-21, 24; 1G-07

CONFLICT OF INTEREST 1A-21, 22, 23; 1C-23
CONTRABAND 3A-18; 4G-07; 5D-06, 07, 08
CONTRACT SERVICES 1A-12; 1B-13; 1C-24; 4C-11

COUNSELING 3D-24
　Availability 4F-03
　Family/parental education 4F-04
　Participation 5A-02
　Program 4F-01

CRIMINAL JUSTICE SYSTEM 1A-02, 05; 1F-03
CRISIS INTERVENTION SERVICES 5C-06
DISCIPLINARY DETENTION (See SEGREGATION)

DISCIPLINARY PROCEDURES (See also RULES OF INMATE CONDUCT; VIOLATIONS)
　Administrative review 3C-21
　Appeal 3C-22
　Corporal punishment (See also DISCIPLINE) 3E-08
　Criminal act 3C-06; 3E-09
　Disciplinary detention (See also SEGREGATION: Disciplinary detention) 3D-01, 04, 07
　Grievance procedure 4G-07
　Hearings 3D-04
　　decision 3C-18
　　hearing record 3C-15, 19
　　inmate participation 3C-06, 12, 16
　　panel 3C-15
　　representation 3C-17
　　schedule 3C-13, 14
　　written notice 3C-11
　Investigation 3C-09
　Mentally ill inmates 4E-38
　Prehearing detention 3C-10
　Reports 3C-07, 08, 11, 20, 21
　Sanctions 3C-03, 04; 3D-07
　　prohibited sanctions 3E-08; 4C-08

DISCIPLINE 3A-31; 3D-06

EDUCATION (See also TRAINING; PERSONNEL: Qualifications)
　Academic/vocational programs 3D-24; 5A-02; 5B-01, 02
　　equipment/facilities 2E-04
　　inmate needs 3D-14
　　postsecondary 5B-01
　　program accreditation 5A-13
　Community resources 1D-05; 5B-02
　Health education 4E-33
　Personnel 1D-10, 21

EMERGENCY PROCEDURES
　Communications 3B-06, 07
　Emergency plans 3B-10, 14
　Emergency repairs plan 3B-08
　Equipment 3B-01, 06, 09
　　power 3B-06, 09
　　testing 3B-01, 09
　Escapes 3B-15
　Evacuation 3B-11, 12
　　drills 3B-11
　　exits 3B-11
　　plans 3B-11
　Firearm distribution 3A-26, 32
　Fire emergencies (See also FIRE SAFETY) 3B-01
　First aid 4E-24, 26
　Medical emergencies (See also HEALTH CARE SERVICES: Emergency care) 4E-23
　Training 3B-10

EQUAL EMPLOYMENT OPPORTUNITIES
　Affirmative action program 1C-07

EVALUATIONS
　Classification 4B-01
　Inspections 1A-17
　Institutional programs 1A-17
　Menu preparation 4C-02
　Performance criteria 1F-06
　Status reports 4E-03
　Training program 1D-02

FIRE SAFETY (See also EMERGENCY PROCEDURES)
　Equipment 3B-01, 06, 09
　Evacuation 3B-10, 11, 12
　　drills 3B-11
　　plan 3B-11
　Exits 3B-11, 12
　Fire drills 3B-11
　Fire prevention plan 3B-01
　Fire safety codes 2A-02; 3B-02, 11
　Inspections 3B-01, 02, 05, 09
　Materials, fire hazards of 2A-02; 3B-03, 05
　　storage 3B-05
　Noncombustible receptacles 3B-04

Index

FISCAL MANAGEMENT
   Accounting system 1B-04, 05, 16; 4C-02
      audits 1B-08, 09, 17
      check and monies control 1B-02, 04, 06, 07
      vouchers 1B-02
   Bonding 1B-02, 15
   Budget 1B-03; 2C-01; 4C-02
      planning 2C-01
      preparation 1B-03; 4C-02
      requests 1B-03
   Commissary 1B-16, 17
   Compensation 1C-20
   Fiscal officer 1B-01
   Inmate funds (See also INMATE PERSONAL PROPERTY) 1B-18, 20
      control of 1B-19; 5D-07
      personal accounts 5D-07
   Insurance 1B-15; 3A-24
   Inventory control 1B-10
   Management 1B-01, 08
   Position control 1B-14
   Purchasing 1B-11, 13; 4C-02
   Service contracts 1A-12; 1B-13
FOOD SERVICE
   Diets, special 4C-06, 07
   Facilities/equipment 2E-07; 4C-09, 14
   Fiscal management 4C-02
   Inmate clothing 4D-09
   Inspection 4C-12, 13
   Meals
      conditions 4C-08, 15
      frequency 4C-16
   Menu 4C-04, 05
   Personnel 4C-01
      foodhandlers 4C-11
      supervisors 4C-01
   Records 4C-03
   Regulations
      dietary allowances 4C-04
      health/safety standards 2E-07, 08; 4C-09, 11, 14
   Storage 2E-07; 4C-14
FORCE, USE OF 1D-17; 3A-17, 28, 31, 32; 3E-08
GRIEVANCE PROCEDURES
   Inmates 3E-11; 4G-07; 5D-06
   Personnel 1C-01
HANDICAPPED, PROVISIONS FOR
   Facilities 2F-03
   Inmates 3E-04; 5A-03, 14, 15, 16, 17
   Work plan 5A-03, 14, 15, 16, 17
HEALTH AUTHORITY (See HEALTH CARE SERVICES)
HEALTH CARE SERVICES
   Access 3D-09; 4E-06, 31
      continuity of care 4E-05, 16
      physical examination 4C-11
      sick call 4E-26
   Coordinator 4E-13
   Death 4E-45
   Dental services 4E-23
      appraisal 4E-19, 20
      emergency 4E-23
      personnel 4E-23
   Diet 4C-06
   Emergency care (See also EMERGENCY PROCEDURES)
      first aid 4E-24, 25
      health care 4E-19, 20, 21, 23, 38
   Facility 4E-08
      equipment 4E-07
   Family notification 4E-44, 45
   Health appraisal 4E-21, 22
   Health authority 4E-01, 02
      policy review 4E-04
      reports 4E-03
      responsibilities 4E-01, 02
   Health education 4E-33
   Hospital care 4E-08
   Infirmary care 4E-08
   Informed consent 4E-42
   Mental health services 4E-11, 12, 37; 5A-02
      housing 4E-37, 38
   Nursing 4E-10
   Orders, direct/standing 4E-10, 11
   Pharmaceutical
      management 4E-17
      psychotropic drugs 4E-18
   Records 4E-46, 47
      transfers 4E-31, 48
   Research 4E-43
   Restraints 4E-18, 32
   Screening 4E-19, 20; 4G-07
   Special care needs 4E-19, 20, 30
      chronic/convalescent 4E-28
      prostheses/orthotic devices 4E-29
      specialists 4E-27
      substance abuse 4E-39, 40; 4F-05
   Staff 3A-19; 4E-09, 10
      health-trained personnel 3A-18; 4E-13, 19, 20, 21
      inmates 4E-16
      licensing 4E-09, 11, 23
      qualified health personnel 4E-19, 20, 21, 22
      students/interns 4E-15
      training 4E-17, 24, 34
   Transfers 4E-20, 24, 30, 31, 34, 38, 48
   Treatment plan 4E-21, 40
HYGIENE
   Inmate clothing 4D-06, 07, 08, 09, 10
      cleaning 4D-10

Index

issue 4D-06, 07, 08, 09
Inspection 4D-01
Linens 4D-06, 07, 11; 4E-24
Personal hygiene 2C-10; 3D-13; 3E-10; 4D-12, 13, 14
  bathing facilities 2C-10
  hair care 3D-14; 3E-10; 4D-14
Water supply 4D-02

INFORMATION DISSEMINATION
Community agencies 1A-05
Confidentiality (See also CONFIDENTIALITY) 1C-24
Media 1A-19
Public information programs 1A-05, 13
Research 1F-09

INFORMATION SYSTEMS (See also PLANNING) 1F-01
Access 1F-01, 02
Collaboration 1F-03
Contribute to 1F-01
Evaluation (See also EVALUATION)
  performance criteria 1F-06
Population statistics 1F-05; 4E-03
Security 1F-02

INMATE MONEY (See also FISCAL MANAGEMENT: Inmate funds) 1B-19, 20

INMATE ORIENTATION (See ADMISSION PROCEDURES)

INMATE PERSONAL PROPERTY (See also ADMISSION PROCEDURES) 2E-11; 4A-04; 4G-07

INMATE RIGHTS
Classification 4F-02
Coeducational institutions 3E-05, 06
Communication
  correspondence 5A-02; 5D-02, 03, 05, 06
  media 1A-19; 3E-07
  telephone 3D-21, 22, 23; 5D-09
Counseling, pregnant inmates 4F-04
Disciplinary procedures (See also DISCIPLINARY PROCEDURES) 3C-11, 13, 14, 15, 16, 17, 19, 22
Discrimination 3E-04; 5A-01, 03, 14, 15, 16, 17
Grievance procedure 3E-11
Health care, access to 4E-01, 05, 06, 23, 26
Healthful environment 3E-04
  food service 4C-04
  physical plant 2A-01, 02; 2C-01, 02, 08, 09, 11, 12; 2D-02, 03, 04, 06, 09; 3B-08
  sanitation/hygiene 4D-01, 04, 05, 08, 11
Legal system, access to
  attorneys 3E-02; 5D-06, 12
  courts 3E-01
  law library 3E-03
  materials 3D-18
Personal abuse 3A-17, 31; 3E-08

Personal grooming 2C-10; 3D-13, 14; 3E-10; 4D-14
Prison number 4E-35
Programs, access to 4E-35
  refusal to participate 5A-02
Recreation 2E-01, 02; 3D-20, 24; 5C-01
Religion 4C-07; 5F-06, 07
Searches, new crime 3E-09
Segregation (See also DISCIPLINARY PROCEDURES)
  conditions 3D-12, 13, 14, 16, 17, 18, 19, 20, 21, 22, 23, 24
  placement in 3D-02, 03, 04, 05
  release 3D-05, 06
Visits (See also VISITATION) 3D-17; 5A-02; 5D-10

INMATE, SPECIAL MANAGEMENT (See SEGREGATION)

INSPECTIONS
Emergency equipment 3B-01, 06, 09
Fire Safety 3B-01, 02, 09
Food Service 4C-12, 13
Industrial/vocational programs 5A-13
Living/activity areas 3A-11, 12
Operations 1A-17
Sanitation 4D-01
Security devices 3A-13
Weapons 3A-32

JUVENILES 4B-04

LEGAL ASSISTANCE
Administration 1A-20
Inmates 3E-03, 04; 4E-09
  materials 3D-18

LIBRARY SERVICES 3D-24; 5A-02; 5E-01, 04
Materials 5E-03, 04
Staffing 5A-02; 5D-01, 02, 04, 06; 5E-02

MAIL SERVICES 5A-02; 5D-01, 02, 04, 06
Censorship 5D-05
Contraband 5D-08
Inspection 5D-07, 08
Postage allowance 5D-03
Segregation 3D-16

MANAGEMENT INFORMATION (See INFORMATION SYSTEMS; RESEARCH)

MEDICAL SERVICES (See HEALTH CARE SERVICES)

MENTAL HEALTH (See HEALTH CARE SERVICES)

PERSONNEL
Benefits 1B-15; 1C-01
  compensation 1C-18
  insurance 1B-15; 3A-24
  reimbursement 1C-20; 1D-09, 21
Code of Ethics 1C-23; 1G-06
Communication 1A-16

Index

Confidentiality (See also CONFIDENTIALITY) 1C-24
Contract personnel 1A-12; 1C-24
Criminal record check 1C-12
Education (See also EDUCATION) 1D-20, 21
Employee/management relations 1C-01
Equal employment opportunities 1C-01
    affirmative action 1C-07
    ex-offenders 1C-25
Force, use of (See also FORCE, USE OF) 3A-05
Grievance procedure 1C-01
Job description 4E-09
Performance review 1C-01, 16; 3D-10
Physical examination 1C-01, 13, 15
Policies 4D-08
    formulation 1A-04
    manual 1C-01, 02
Political involvement 1A-21; 1C-23
Post orders 3A-05, 06
Probationary period 1C-05
Promotion 1C-08, 10
Qualifications 1A-08, 09; 1C-01, 08; 3C-11; 3D-10; 4C-10; 4E-09, 11; 5F-01, 02
    education 1A-09
    experience 1A-09; 4C-01
    licensure/certification 4E-09, 11
Records 1C-21, 22
Reports 1A-21, 22, 23; 3D-11
Responsibilities 1A-08
Salaries 1C-01
Segregation 3D-10
Selection (See also Criminal record check; Physical examination) 1C-08
Staff participation 1A-04; 3D-19
Staffing requirements 1B-14; 1C-03
    emergency staffing 1C-11
    needs assessment 1C-05
    vacancy rate 1C-06
Supervisors
    duties 3A-11, 12, 13; 3B-14
    programs 1D-01; 1G-01; 3D-02, 09; 4C-01; 4E-13; 5E-02; 5F-01, 02
Termination 1A-08, 10; 1C-01
    hearings 1A-10
Training (See TRAINING)
Weapons, use of (See TRAINING; WEAPONS, USE OF)
Work stoppage 3B-13
PHYSICAL PLANT
    Administrative facilities 2F-01, 02
    Architectural barriers 2C-13; 2F-03
    Capacity
        cell capacity 2C-01
        institution 2B-02, 03
        multiple-occupancy rooms 2C-01
        rated bed capacity 2B-04

Dayroom 2C-05, 07
Exercise space 2E-01
Fire safety (See also EMERGENCY PROCEDURES; FIRE SAFETY)
    evacuation 3B-12
    exits 3B-12
    finishing material 2A-02; 3B-03
Floor space requirements
    dayroom 2C-06
    exercise space 2E-01, 02
    multiple-occupancy 2C-01
    single-occupancy 2C-01, 11, 12; 2D-03
Furnishings 2C-01, 02, 08, 09, 11, 12; 2D-02, 03, 04, 06, 09; 3B-03
Inspections (See also INSPECTIONS) 3A-13; 3B-02; 4D-10; 5A-13
Lighting requirements 2C-01, 02, 08, 09, 11, 12; 2D-01, 02, 03, 05, 06, 07, 09
Location (new only) 2B-05
Maintenance 3B-08
    cleaning equipment 2E-09, 10
    housekeeping plan 4D-05
Multiple-occupancy rooms 2C-01
    dormitories 2C-01
National code compliance
    building codes 2A-01
    fire safety codes 2A-02; 3B-11
    sanitation/health codes 4C-09; 4D-01, 02; 4E-08
Noise levels 2C-01, 02, 08, 09, 11; 2D-02, 03, 04, 06, 09
Program facilities
    educational programs 2E-04
    food services 4C-09
    recreation activities 2C-06, 07; 2E-01; 5C-02
    religious services 5F-09, 10
    training 1D-08
    visiting 2E-03; 5D-11
Sanitation facilities 2C-01, 02, 08, 09, 11, 12; 2D-02, 03, 04, 06, 09; 2E-08
    bathing facilities 2C-10
Segregation 2C-11, 12; 2D-03; 2E-02
Service facilities
    commissary 2E-13
    food service 2E-06, 08
    health care service 4E-08
Space management 3B-08
Storage space
    inmate 2C-01; 2E-11
    mechanical equipment 2E-12
    linens 2E-10
Temperatures 2C-01, 02, 08, 09, 11, 12; 2D-02, 03, 04, 06, 09
Watchtowers 2G-02
PLANNING (See also INFORMATION SYSTEMS) 2C-01

Index

Budgeting 2C-01
Community involvement 1A-05
Objectives 1A-03
Workload formula 2E-04, 05
POLICY (See ADMINISTRATION: Policy and procedure)
PRIVACY (See CONFIDENTIALITY)
PROGRAMS (See also EDUCATION; INFORMATION DISSEMINATION: Public information programs; RECREATION ACTIVITIES; RELIGIOUS SERVICES; WORK PROGRAMS)
   Assignment
      classification 3A-16, 18
      mentally ill 4E-38
      program status review 4B-02
   Availability 3D-24; 3E-05
   Budgeting 1B-03; 2C-01
   Coeducational 3E-05
   Evaluation 1A-17
   Health education 4E-33
   Management 2C-01
   Participation 5A-02
   Purchase of services 1B-13
   Training program 1D-01
PROTECTIVE CUSTODY (See SEGREGATION)
RECEPTION (See ADMISSION PROCEDURES)
RECORDS
   Case records (See also CASE RECORDS) 1E-01
   Confidentiality
      case records 1E-01, 05
      personnel 1C-21
   Food service 4C-02
   Health care records (See also HEALTH CARE SERVICES) 4E-47, 48
   Master file 1F-04
   Personnel (See also PERSONNEL) 1C-21, 22
   Population movement 1F-05
RECREATION ACTIVITIES
   Availability 3D-24; 5C-01
   Equipment 5C-02
   Exercise 2E-01, 02; 3D-20
   Facilities
      dayroom 2C-06, 07; 2E-01
      exercise space 2C-06; 2E-01; 3C-13;
   Inmate activities 3C-15
   Participation 5A-02
RELEASE PREPARATION
   Graduated release 4G-05
   Procedures 4G-07
   Program 4G-01, 02, 03, 04
   Participation 5A-02
RELIGIOUS SERVICES
   Availability 3D-05, 24
   Chaplains 5F-04, 05
   Equipment/facilities 5F-09

   Participation 5A-02
   Religious freedom 3E-04; 4C-07; 5F-08
   Staffing 5F-01
REPORTS
   Commissary 1B-17
   Disciplinary 3C-07, 08, 11, 20
   Inspection 3A-13
   Line staff 3A-10, 11
   Health care 4E-03
   Parent agency, reports to 1A-18; 1B-07, 08
   Special incidents 3A-10, 31; 3D-15
RESEARCH (See also CONFIDENTIALITY; INFORMATION SYSTEMS)
   Approval 1F-10
   Conduct of 1F-09, 10
   Evaluation (See also EVALUATION) 1A-17; 1F-06
   Information dissemination (See also INFORMATION DISSEMINATION) 1F-09
   Information storage 1F-01
   Inmate participation 1F-11; 4E-42
RULES OF INMATE CONDUCT (See also DISCIPLINARY PROCEDURES) 3C-01, 04
   Rulebook 3C-03
SANITATION
   Housekeeping plan 4D-05
   Inspection (See also INSPECTIONS) 4D-01
   Personnel 4D-05
   Pest control 4D-04
   Regulations 4D-01, 02
   Waste disposal 4D-03
   Water supply 4D-02
SEARCHES 3A-18, 19, 20; 3E-09; 4A-01; 5D-15
SECURITY AND CONTROL
   Chemical agents 1D-19; 2G-04; 3A-25, 27
   Communications 2G-01; 3B-07
   Contraband 3A-18; 4E-10, 11, 12
   Control center 2G-01; 3A-02
   Emergency situations 3B-07, 12, 14
      plans 3B-10
   Equipment control 3A-22; 3B-05
   Escapes 3A-31; 3B-15
   Evacuation 3B-11, 12
   Evaluation 1F-06
   Force, use of 1D-17; 3A-17, 28, 29, 31, 32; 3E-08
   Hostages 1C-01; 3B-14
   Injuries 3A-29
   Inmate count 1F-05; 3A-14
   Inmate movement 1F-05; 3A-15
   Inmate transportation 3A-16, 17; 4E-31, 32
   Inspection
      equipment 2G-04; 3A-27
      facility 3A-11, 12
      security devices 3A-13
   Key control 3A-21; 3B-12
   Log 3A-10

Index

Manual 3A-01
Patrols 3A-11
Perimeter 1E-05; 2G-02, 03; 3A-32
Post orders 3A-05, 06
Reports 3A-11, 13, 28, 31
Restraints 3A-17; 4E-32
Safety vestibule 2G-03
Sallyports 2G-03
Search procedures 3A-18, 19, 20; 3E-09; 4A-02
Security devices
    emergency 3A-26
    inspection 2G-04; 3A-13, 27, 32
    record of use 3A-26
    restraints 3A-17; 4E-32
    storage 2G-04; 3A-27
    use of 3A-25, 28
Special units 1D-16
Staff accessibility 3A-14
Staff training 1D-12, 13, 16; 2G-02; 3A-20; 3B-10
Supervisors (See also PERSONNEL: Supervisors; SUPERVISORY STAFF) 4B-02
Unit management 2B-02, 03
Vehicles 3A-23, 24
Watchtowers 2G-02; 3A-32
Weapons, use of 2G-02; 3A-25, 30, 32
    reports 1D-21
    training 1D-18
Work stoppage 3B-13
SEGREGATION
    Administrative segregation
        classification 4B-02
        physical plant 2E-02
        placement procedures 3C-10
        program access 3D-24
        status review 3C-10; 3D-05, 06
        telephone privileges 3D-22
    Disciplinary detention
        duration 3D-07
        placement procedures 4E-45
        telephone privileges 3D-23
    Exercise 2E-01, 02; 3D-20
    Inmate rights (See also INMATE RIGHTS) 3E-11
    Legal materials 3D-18; 3E-03
    Mail 3D-16
    Medical services (See also MEDICAL SERVICES) 3D-09
    Meals 4C-08
    Operational policy and procedure 3D-01, 02
    Personal hygiene 3D-13, 14
    Personal items 3D-12
    Personnel 3D-10
    Physical plant (See also PHYSICAL PLANT) 2C-11, 12; 2D-03
    Privileges, deprivation of 3D-15
    Protective custody
        placement procedures 3D-03
        program access 3D-24
        telephone privileges 3D-21
    Reading materials 3D-19
    Records 3D-11
    Staff access 3D-09
    Visitation 3D-17; 5D-10
SOCIAL SERVICES 3D-24; 4F-02
    Availability 3D-24
    Counseling (See also COUNSELING) 4F-03
    Crisis intervention 4F-03
    Family/parental education 4F-04
    Inmate needs 4F-01
    Participation 5A-02
    Substance abuse program 4F-05
SPECIAL NEEDS INMATES 4B-03; 4E-28, 37, 39
SUBSTANCE ABUSE 4E-39, 41; 4F-05
SUPERINTENDENT (See WARDEN/SUPERINTENDENT)
SUPERVISORY STAFF
    Meetings 1A-16
    Responsibilities 3A-15
    Training 1D-12
    Work stoppage 3B-13
TELEPHONE PRIVILEGES 3D-21, 22, 23; 5D-09
TEMPORARY RELEASE 3A-14; 4G-04, 06; 5D-14
TRAINING (See also EDUCATION)
    Advisory committee 1D-07
    Chemical agents, use of 1D-19
    Force, use of 1D-17
    Inmates (See also EDUCATION: Academic/vocational programs)
        literacy training 5B-01
    Library services 1D-03, 04, 05
    Orientation 1D-15; 1G-06
    Part-time employee 1G-09
    Professional involvement 1D-21
    Program personnel
        chaplain 5F-01
    Reference services 1D-03, 04, 05
    Reimbursement 1D-09, 10, 21
    Specialized training
        administration/management 1D-13
        chemical agents 1D-19
        emergency plans 3B-10
        emergency unit 1D-16
        health care 3A-19, 20; 4E-17, 24
        management information system 1F-02
        rules of inmate conduct 3C-04
        self-defense 1D-17
        watchtower duty 2G-02
        weapons 1D-18; 3A-32
    Training hours
        administrative/managerial staff 1D-13
        clerical/support personnel 1D-11

correctional officers 1D-12
emergency unit officers 1D-16
support personnel 1D-14
Training program 1D-01
equipment 1D-08
evaluation 1D-02
facilities 1D-08
staff 1D-01, 07
supervisor 1D-01
Volunteers 1G-06
Weapons, use of 1D-18; 3A-32
TRANSFERS, INMATE
Case records 1E-02
Health records 4E-48
Medical screening 4E-20
Medical transfers 4E-30
mental illness 4E-38
procedures 4E-24, 31
Transportation 3A-16, 17; 4E-32
VIOLATIONS (See also DISCIPLINARY PROCEDURES; RULES OF INMATE CONDUCT) 3C-02, 09; 3D-04, 07
Criminal behavior 3E-09
Criminal prosecution 3C-06
Inmate rules 3C-01, 03, 04
Minor misbehavior 3C-05
Staff training 3C-04
VISITATION 3D-17; 5A-02
Extended visits 5D-13
Facilities 5D-11
Furloughs 5D-14
High-risk inmates 5D-11
Limitations 5D-10
Physical contact 5D-11
Special visits 5D-12
Transportation 5D-16
Visitor requirements 5D-15
VOCATIONAL EDUCATION (See EDUCATION)
VOLUNTEERS
Policies 1A-15
Qualifications 1G-05
Schedule 1G-08
Selection 1G-03
Training 1G-06
Volunteer service program 1G-01, 02, 04, 07, 09
WARDEN/SUPERINTENDENT
Appointments 1A-06, 07, 09, 10
Qualifications 1A-08, 09
Responsibilities
approval required 1F-10; 3A-17, 25; 3D-02, 07; 3E-09; 4E-38
fiscal management 1B-01, 03
hearings 3C-21
inmate contact 3A-12
inspections 1A-17; 3A-12

meetings 1A-16; 4E-03
mission statement 1A-03
operations 1A-17
outside agencies 1A-12
personnel 1A-06; 1C-02
reports received 3A-28; 4E-03
reviews 1C-02; 1F-10; 3C-10, 21; 3D-07
segregation 1E-01
Termination 1A-08, 10
Term of office 1A-10
Training 1D-13
Staff communication 1A-16
WEAPONS, USE OF 2G-02; 3A-25, 32
Reports 3A-28
Training 1D-18
WORK PROGRAMS 5A-01
Conduct of 5A-06, 11, 12, 13
Experience 5A-06
Job assignments 4E-16; 5A-01, 06, 07
Handicapped 5A-03
Inmate clothing 4D-09
Inspections 5A-13
Participation 5A-02
Payment 5A-18, 19
Resources 5A-11
WORK STOPPAGE 3B-13

ACA File No._____

PROPOSAL FOR STANDARD REVISION

Manual_____Edition_____Date_____
Standard Number_____
☐ New Standard   ☐ Deletion
☐ Revision   ☐ Interpretation

Existing Standard (Insert complete standard and discussion.) _____
_____
_____
_____
_____
_____
_____
_____

Proposal (State the standard and discussion exactly as you believe it should appear in the manual. Proposal must be in the same format and worded precisely.) _____
_____
_____
_____
_____
_____
_____
_____

Rationale for revision (Attach additional information if required.) _____
_____
_____
_____
_____
_____
_____
_____

Proposed by:

Signature _____
Title   _____
Agency   _____
City   _____State____Zip_____
Phone   _____

Forward to:
American Correctional Association
Department of Standards and Accreditation
4380 Forbes Blvd.
Lanham, MD 20706-4322